In this end-time season, it is absolutely critical that the arrows of intercession we shoot hit the mark all the time. The prophet Jeremiah spoke these words: "Yes, prepare to attack Babylon, all you nations round about. Let your archers shoot at her. Spare no arrows, for she has sinned against the Lord" (Jer. 50:14). I personally found it amazing that the Lord has released Dr. Charles Robinson to publish this book in his fiftieth year, and also finalized it in 2014; this further confirms the passage for me. Through this book, the Lord is giving us some very specific targets at which we need to shoot, because it's time for the enemy's systems to be brought down.

This is a book for every agent God has raised up to bring about the cultural transformation of nations. Charles and Liz have played a major intercessory role in my personal journey, using many of the treasures that are shared in the *Let Heaven Invade the Seven Mountains of Culture: 7M Leadership Certification Guide*.

— Patrick Kuwana
Founder, Crossover Transformation Group
Johannesburg, South Africa

In this book, Dr. Robinson has pushed forward the concept of spiritual services as a powerful, essential ministry. The manual is packed with practical insights, wisdom, and proven processes. Any leader considering this ministry would do well to read this training manual.

— Dave Kahle
speaker, trainer, executive round table leader
author of *How to Sell Anything to Anyone Anytime* and numerous other works

Endorsements

Leaders need a team that can support their calling through intercession. Charles and Liz have been longtime friends and trusted intercessors for our work. I highly recommend Charles, Liz, and WISE as a valuable addition to any organization that wants to ensure that the spiritual foundation of its calling is secure.

— Os Hillman
President, Marketplace Leaders
author of *Change Agent*, "TGIF-Today God Is First," and other works

I have been researching, writing about, and leading prayer movements for twenty-five years, and I stand amazed at the ways that God has been moving prayer leaders into exciting new areas of effective intercession. Outstanding among them are Charles and Liz Robinson, who have been breaking new ground in the area of professional level intercession. Charles's comprehensive training manual will show how you, as a leader, can benefit from this captivating and kingdom-impacting ministry. You will be glad you have this book, and you will be glad to have read it!

— C. Peter Wagner
Vice President, Global Spheres, Inc.
author of *Warfare Prayer*, *Acts of the Holy Spirit*, and other works

Dr. Charles and Elizabeth Robinson are ordained ministers under Christian International. They have always been passionate about their roles as ministers in the marketplace, and they have now put together a tangible manual in order to help leaders fulfill their God-given assignments in the seven mountains of culture. In the manual *Let Heaven Invade the Seven Mountains of Culture: 7M Leadership Certification Guide*, the Robinsons have gone deep in sharing their wisdom to equip and help leaders fulfill their mandates through their enterprises.

— Bishop Bill Hamon
Founder, Christian International Ministries Network
author of *The Eternal Church*, *The Day of the Saints*, and other works

I really believe in what Charles and Liz Robinson are doing, and this book describes the how-tos of a kingdom service that can really be of significant value for those arising on the mountains of society; it will help equip them for success.

— Johnny Enlow
author of *The Seven Mountain Prophecy* and other works

Combining proven intercessory practices of the past, Charles has added a strategic prophetic focus that will launch a new level of intercession and kingdom advancement for leaders from all walks of life. Those who utilize these concepts will bring spiritual ministry to a higher plane of freshness and impact. May a new generation of marketplace ministers arise!

— Randy DeMain
President, Kingdom Revelation Ministries

Dr. Charles and Liz Robinson, in *Let Heaven Invade the Seven Mountains of Culture: 7M Leadership Certification Guide,* have been leaders in exposing what God is doing to his businesses at this time with his apostles and intercessors. The link with the seven mountains, and use of an accreditation process, shows an advanced entrepreneurial flair which the body of Christ needs to embrace.

God is a businessman, and he expects us to develop the skills to bring his kingdom from heaven to earth as we pray in the Lord's Prayer. We are told many are perishing through lack of knowledge of the ways of the Father. The devil has been the one deceiving and lying to the elect wherever he can, and causing the body of Christ to be ineffective.

The roles of business apostles and professional intercessors are still very controversial in church structures today. Accreditation and commissioning is helpful—to not only the businesses they serve, but also to being confirmed in these roles. We all can easily be discouraged before the fruit appears. We need to honor and love each other's gifting and glorify God through this.

— Dr. Stan Jeffery
Founder, Boardroom Prophets
CEO, Christ in Business Ventures, Sydney, Australia

LET HEAVEN INVADE
THE SEVEN MOUNTAINS OF CULTURE

BECOME
A SEVEN MOUNTAINS
LEADER

DR. CHARLES ROBINSON

↑SPIRIT-LED
⤴PUBLISHING

Let Heaven Invade The Seven Mountains of Culture
Become a Seven Mountains Leader

Copyright © 2014 by WISE Ministries International
All rights reserved. No part of this publication may be reproduced, distributed, or transmitted in any form or by any means, including photocopying, recording, or other electronic or mechanical methods, without the prior written permission of the publisher, except in the case of brief quotations embodied in critical reviews and certain other noncommercial uses permitted by copyright law. For permission requests, write to the author, addressed "Attention: Permissions," at the e-mail address below:

Dr. Charles Robinson
info@coachmybusiness.com

Special discounts are available on quantity purchases by corporations, associations, and others. Orders by US trade bookstores and wholesalers—for details, contact the author at the e-mail address above.

Scripture quotations are from THE HOLY BIBLE, NEW INTERNATIONAL VERSION®, NIV® Copyright © 1973, 1978, 1984, 2011 by Biblica, Inc.® Used by permission. All rights reserved worldwide.

Editing team: Say It Well! & Inksnatcher
Cover design team: Inksnatcher & Allison Metcalfe Design
Photo of Dr. Charles Robinson: Allison Metcalfe Photography

First Edition, 2014
ISBN: 978-0-9904902-4-1
Publisher: Spirit-Led Publishing

I dedicate this second work to all the leaders who have been equipped and empowered through the truths presented in this guide. Thank you for opening up your lives so that we could engage both earthly and heavenly solutions and help launch the spiritual services industry together.

I also dedicate this manual to our own spiritual advisory team — without whom this work could not go forward.

Acknowledgements

Special thanks to Cathy Buettner's writing services at Say It Well! for guiding me with grace and patience on a compressed timetable. Your generosity with your Spirit-led anointing in reorganization, training, editing, and marketplace ministry transformed this work. Cathy, you are a gem!

Special gratitude to Fred and Dorinda Trick, and to all our clients and friends. Your partnerships and friendships have impacted Liz and me in ways that only God knows. This work is a testimony to the lessons learned by each of us as we have worked together.

We thank Sally Hanan of Inksnatcher, who has been a divine connection to make the final preparations on the manuscript for publishing. Your knowledge of the publishing industry and your skillsets are broad and amazing; you quickly produced excellent results. Thank you for blessing this kingdom assignment with your work.

We also thank Allison Metcalfe of Allison Metcalfe Photography and Design for how she seamlessly integrated with Inksnatcher to design and format this book's cover and interior and to insert, redo, or acquire graphics as needed to enhance the text. Her attention to detail and eye for beauty have brought these words up higher.

Table of Contents

Forward

Preface

1. Support & Empowerment
2. Find, Engage, Release
3. Executive Coaching
4. Favor & Breakthrough
5. Spiritual Services
6. Spiritual Coaching
7. A 7M-Enabled Leader
8. Strategic Intelligence
9. Your Choices

About the Author

More from WISE

Foreword

God is speaking to many in the church today about the role of the seven cultural mountains of influence and how strategic they are to influencing the culture for Jesus Christ. What was birthed in 1975 through Bill Bright, of Campus Crusade, and Loren Cunningham, of Youth With a Mission, is just now being realized as a core strategy to influence the culture.

We have learned that it only takes 3-5 percent of leadership operating at the top of one of these cultural spheres to actually shift the mountain—as evidenced by the gay rights movement, which has shifted the public's view of its issue by using arts & entertainment and media to reframe the public's view of it.

One of the important ingredients to this new strategy focus is the spiritual services required to prepare the soil for effective ministry to these seven areas. Charles Robinson, in the second volume of his new work, *Let Heaven Invade the Seven Mountains of Culture,* has given us a new resource tool for those called to lead and use their influence in the seven cultural mountains.

The Lord tells us that is it "not by might, nor by power, but by my Spirit." Prayer must be at the forefront. Ezekiel 22:30 tells us that God is looking for someone to stand in the gap so that the land might not be destroyed. This book will help you understand God's prayer strategy to affect the seven cultural mountains.

I highly recommend this resource to help you become a spiritually sound and mighty leader to affect the seven cultural mountains, so that we can restore the biblical foundations of this great nation and positively affect the nations of the world.

—Os Hillman
President, Marketplace Leaders
author of *Change Agent,* "TGIF-Today God Is First," and other works

Preface

"Those who are wise will shine like the brightness of the heavens, and those who lead many to righteousness, like the stars for ever and ever" (Daniel 12:3).

Three Assumptions I Make as I Write This for You

Assumption 1: You are a Christian and that means, for our discussion, that you have received Christ into your heart, consider yourself born again, and that you have been water baptized.

Assumption 2: You are a leader in one of the seven mountains of culture and you desire to become all that you are called by God to be.

Assumption 3: You will just skip forward if the marketing language in this manual turns you off. My function in WISE has been as an intercessor, sales, and marketing consultant, and as the first coach to our clients (we have since added other coaches). A portion of the book markets WISE and our associated endeavors. However, I do this because it can only help you, my reader, to receive a full impartation of the spirit of what we are accomplishing in the marketplace. As such, I recommend that you read everything in its entirety.

Who Is This Guide For?

This guide was written to impart spiritual truth to leaders who desire to include God in every detail of their enterprises, as well as for those who desire to avail themselves of every spiritual advantage to be victorious and empowered for success. We will focus in this guide on the spiritual advisory/support team roles of intercessor, coach, corporate pastor, and chief revelatory officer (CRO). We'll highlight how to identify, engage, manage, and release these individuals for your corporate, familial, and personal well-being.

The Importance of Spiritual Support

You are a Christian leader in the seven mountains and especially in business, so you are the tip of the spear. God uses you to pierce dark structures, take territory away from the ruler of the kingdom of darkness, and win that territory over to the kingdom of light. As a leader in your sphere, you are surrounded by perceived and imperceived spiritual warfare. God wants to illuminate the darkness that is trying to engulf you and your enterprise. Scripture declares that we are not ignorant of the enemy's devices. God has given us our weapons of warfare, which are the gifts of Holy Spirit as outlined in I Corinthians 12 and 14.

You need to be supported.

Before addressing the benefits of a spiritual advisory or support team, I need to affirm that you are the first and best line of defense against the wiles and onslaught of the enemy. We all need help and assistance in our callings, and in our assignments from God, but unless we guard our hearts and minds—our temples—others cannot help as much. They are much better at helping ward off attacks that come from outside the temple.

We are responsible to guard our own temples—the Holy of Holies, if you will—but we also need individuals who minister to us one-on-one (deliverance minsters, counselors, prophets, etc.). These ministry times are very valuable to our personal growth, emotions, and spirits.

The spiritual support team (SAT) is your shield of defense.

It's also your offensive spiritual thrust for you, your family, your leaders, and your enterprise. Your enterprise has a destiny that the SAT helps to ensure you're on track with: Your enterprise needs to be where God wants it to be and do what God desires for it to do. It should impact the markets, nations, and territories God has destined it to impact.

How Does God View My Enterprise?

Your organization cannot be saved, but it can be sanctified—set apart for the use of the Master and the kingdom. Your enterprise can also be an impenetrable fortress of God and a force for good. Finally, your enterprise can also be a storehouse of mysteries—patents, intellectual property, and other intangible assets—and financial assets, such as lands, buildings, and other resources.

Think of yourself as a modern-day Joseph, as outlined in the book of Genesis, second only to Pharaoh and over all that Egypt possessed. In the same way that Joseph directed the mass storage of grain in preparation for the seven lean years, is God calling you to store up provision for his people for the coming years of lack? What part does your enterprise play in this?

Support & Empowerment

"Most intercession is in the religion mountain. How are leaders in the other six mountains to get the necessary intercession? Charles Robinson's company: WISE (Workplace Intercession, Support, Empowerment)"

— Apostle C. Peter Wagner
Vice President, Global Spheres, Inc.
author of *Warfare Prayer*, *Acts of the Holy Spirit* and other works

"Dr. Charles and Elizabeth Robinson have a unique perspective concerning ministry in the marketplace. Prior to their training and ordination into the ministry through Christian International, under the headship of Bishop Bill Hamon, they operated successfully in the business world and are now taking their wealth of experience to the marketplace.

As founders and originators of WISE Ministry, the Robinsons' organization provides Christian counsel and prayer covering to numerous businesses worldwide."

— Apostle Vance D. Russell,
Founder, Arise Ministries International
author of *The Kingdom* and other works

1

"In the last days the mountain of the Lord's temple will be established as the highest of the mountains; it will be exalted above the hills, and all nations will stream to it" (Isaiah 2:2).

In 1975 Bill Bright, founder of Campus Crusade, and Loren Cunningham, founder of Youth With A Mission, had supper together at a conference and agreed to meet the following morning for breakfast. That night, God simultaneously gave these change agents the same dream, which they shared with each other over breakfast the following day. They saw seven mountains, which formed a larger, single mountain. God said that if they claimed the seven mountains, he would give them the large mountain, which is the kingdom of God.

The message was that if we were to impact any nation for Jesus Christ, then we would have to affect the seven spheres or mountains of society, which are the pillars of any society. These seven mountains are business, government, media, arts and entertainment, education, the family, and religion. (There are many subgroups under these main categories.) About a month later, the Lord showed Francis Schaeffer the same thing. In essence, God was telling these three change agents where the battlefield was. Here was where culture would be won or lost. Their assignment was to raise up change agents to scale the mountains and help a new generation of change agents understand the larger story.

— Os Hillman

Intercession - What Is an Intercessor's Assignment?

A business should always be about God's business, and God's priority is always about the hearts and souls of his people and their relationships with him.

> *When business people are in line with God's heart, then the business will succeed. The closer one walks with the Lord, the easier it is to hear his heartbeat.*

Our prayer is for business owners, their families, and employees to learn to hear his heartbeat and know him in a deeper way.

On the following page there is chart that breaks down an intercessor's assignment. Keep in mind that this is an abridged list, and the Lord will lead you into how and when he wants your intercessor to intercede.

The Issachar anointing

The Issachar anointing is based on I Chron. 12:32, which states [of the numbers of the men armed for battle], "From Issachar, men who understood the times and knew what Israel should do—200 chiefs, with all their relatives under their command." In this hour, God is again raising up anointed men and women who know how to touch heaven and bring the wisdom from above down to earth on behalf of those greatly beloved by God—his businessmen, businesswomen, and leaders in all seven mountains or spheres of society.

An Intercessor's Assignment

The intercessor will:

discover God's vision and desire for both the intercessor and the client,

ask God for his strategy—how he wants to accomplish his vision,

report God's strategy to his overseers,

pray for provision and financial protection, and

pray for emotional, physical, spiritual, moral, relational, and leadership protection.

The intercessor:

partners with God and moves in faith to help bring God into the business,

helps the owner fulfill God's plan and vision for his or her business,

prays for the people's hearts to unite with God's heart,

partners with God and declares God's success, even when he or she does not see it.

The intercessor commits to daily:

walk in obedience to God's holy Word,

walk in purity and seek to be in unity with God, fellow brothers, and sisters in Christ,

walk in forgiveness, confession, and repentance with everyone (Ps. 51),

not allow roots of pride, bitterness, unforgiveness, or rejection to develop in his soul,

put on the whole armor of God (Eph. 6),

proclaim and exercise his authority in Jesus's name, and

proclaim God's promises in his Word for each business's employees and workplace.

He is calling these anointed men and women to bring God's presence, power, and revelation to leaders outside the four walls of the church and into the marketplace. These anointed men and women, as intercessors, will lead the charge in rallying around the leaders in all seven mountains or spheres. Their intercession will help surround, protect, and free the leaders from all kinds of bondages and hindrances, and release them into their respective destinies.

> "From Issachar, men who understood the times and knew what Israel should do—200 chiefs, with all their relatives under their command."
> — 1 Chron. 12:32

Empowering You for Success

The sons of Issachar would go to war for the other tribes in a heartbeat. They rose early and awakened the other tribes with the sound of the shofar.[1]

Issachar tribe members, whose name means "wages" in the original Hebrew, were the donkey or burden bearers of their brothers. Issachar intercessors and coaches have ability in praying for finances. We have seen tremendous financial breakthroughs for our clients from our prayers, time and time again (and even before we start praying, like the time the client's company doubled in size within twenty-four hours of signing the contract!). Can you see how your intercessors' prayers can work so powerfully on your behalf?

> *He is calling these anointed men and women to bring his presence, his power, and his revelation to <u>you</u>.*

As Christians, we can personally pray and apply the words from Christ's prayer "your kingdom come … on earth as it is in heaven." We see an interesting corroboration of the spiritual principle in action from author John Carlson,* who relates the meanings of the names of the twelve tribes listed on the gates to New Jerusalem (in Revelation). We can assume that the presence of their names means something to our Lord, since he never wastes words in his Word. Carlson shares that because the name Issachar can indicate intercession—seen both in the words spoken at the child's birth and the blessing Jacob gave to Issachar—intercession can allow us to enter God's kingdom and to take others in with us. The gate of intercession allows us in and Jesus, himself, will intercede through us.

As Christ was to the multitudes, a multitude of priests will be to the world. This is a level of the unprecedented power and authority of Christ, himself, filling the earth with God's knowledge "as the waters cover the seas" (Hab. 2:14).

Jesus is, of course, the full embodiment of this priesthood.

Types of Intercessors

There are twelve types of intercessors based on the type of anointing they carry:

List intercessor – your personality is orderly and precise; you are faithful in completing commitments and enjoy daily covering a list in its entirety.

Personal intercessor – individuals' personal needs and one-on-one interactions motivate you.

---

* In his book, *Passion for His Presence, Entering His Gates*

 *Worship intercessor* – you enter into the presence of God and wage warfare in the heavenlies through adoration of the Trinity.

 *Crisis intercessor* – when you hear of accidents, tragedies, or other crises that either could happen imminently or have already transpired, something on the inside of you rises up to take action and intervene.

 *People group intercessor* – you feel compelled to intercede for certain cultures or alienated or suppressed groups, to enter into their struggles.

 *Financial intercessor* – you are a person motivated by the need to see God's provision in people's lives or situations; you have a proven ability to see breakthrough in your own and other people's finances.

 *Governmental intercessor* – righteousness and justice motivate you; you are a person who honors our governmental leaders.

Mercy intercessor – you are motivated by (even unwarranted) compassion for people and their needs and failings; you weep easily over people's faults, weaknesses, and infirmities.

Issues intercessor – social causes and their injustices often anger or upset you, causing you to fervently pray.

Soul intercessor – you are outreach oriented; God uses you to bring many to him.

Warfare intercessor – conflict with the enemy excites you (this anointing is strongly related to that of a worship intercessor); you like Scriptures that talk about the vengeance of God on the head of the enemy; you find the need to walk or pace rather than sit or kneel during prayer.

Prophetic intercessor – God gives you information about other people, situations, or events; you frequently receive mental pictures about people, places, or things; what you say often comes to pass.

WISE

When God led us to form WISE™, which stands for "Workplace Intercession, Support, and Empowerment," he let us know that

WISE was going to empower leaders and their employees in the marketplace by helping them fulfill their callings in their businesses and other enterprises. God gave me (Charles) a corporate anointing and let me know:

> He wanted us to take his presence and power outside the four walls of the church and into the marketplace.
>
> He was going to use our business, entrepreneurial, management, and leadership skills to let heaven invade the seven mountains of culture.

God has since let us know that the "Issachar anointing" was going to be in operation in WISE, and that he was going to partner the religion mountain with all of the other mountains to:

> fund the end-time harvest through bringing his modern-day Josephs' wisdom and discernment to multitudes, and
>
> empower his people on the seven mountains for success (the inspiration for our WISE slogan: "Empowering you for success").

Our Background

At the time of this writing, we (Charles and Liz) have brought the word of the Lord to thousands of people. As experienced church and corporate pastors, intercessors, chaplains, teachers, and business owners, we and our team of intercessors and business consultants are equipped to support and empower you and your ministry for success. In 2005 we founded a dynamic local church in Austin, Texas, where we served together as senior pastors for five years.

We are now corporate pastors to many organizations, both nationally and internationally, empowering them to impact all seven mountains of influence. We are committed to, and passionate about, training and imparting the wisdom, understanding, and experience the Lord has given us.

Our mission is to develop strong, mature ambassadors and warriors for Christ, and to bring the saving knowledge of Jesus Christ to our nation and the nations of his world.

One of the ways we do that is through our four certification courses in a series called "Let Heaven Invade the Seven Mountains of Culture."

Course Schedule and Format Options

Certification courses happen monthly. Find them here:
- markteplaceintercessors.com, marketplaceceos.com,
- marketplacecoaches.com, marketplacegenerals.com,
- and/or corporatepastors.com

Both the group and independent study formats offered give the student impartation, wisdom, and experience from personal contact with WISE instructors.

We want to impart spiritual truth to those individuals who feel a call to the ministry of intercession and/or coaching. We want to help leaders in all spheres (especially those in business) fulfill their divine callings from God and engage the valuable services of professional intercessors and coaches.

My Prayer for You!

I pray for your seven mountains leader, Lord, that you would bless him (or her) and give him favor in the mountains and marketplaces that you have called him to. Lord, help your leader to grow his enterprise and launch out in faith into the deep.

God, I pray for a special impartation of the sevenfold Spirit of God, according to Isaiah 11:2-4: "The Spirit of the Lord will rest on him—the Spirit of wisdom and of understanding, the Spirit of counsel and of might, the Spirit of the knowledge and fear of the Lord—he will not judge by what he sees with his eyes, or decide by what he hears with his ears; but with righteousness he will judge the needy, with justice he will give decisions for the poor of the earth."

I pray that every God-given word in this course would be planted deep inside your leader and be recalled when he needs it. Lord, I pray that every ability and anointing I have would now descend upon your leader and that he would do greater works than me.

Lord, I pray for my leader's family and spouse, and for the people in his life who need protection, healing, deliverance, and who need to know someone cares and has their backs. I pray that you would open the windows of heaven right now over the leader's life and ministry, in the name of Jesus, amen!

Module 1: Endnotes

1. DeMain, Randy. "God is Moving Again with Holy Fire – His Manifest Presence is Coming Upon the Priesthood." www.elijahlist.com/words/display_word.html?ID=12660 (accessed June 18, 2014).

Recommended Additional Resources for Leaders

Books

> Wagner, C. Peter. *Prayer Shield: How to Intercede for Pastors, Christian Leaders and Others on the Spiritual Frontlines* Prayer Warrior Series (Book 2)
>
> Carlson, John. *Passion for His Presence, Entering His Gates*
>
> Servello, PR Mike, *God's Shield of Protection*
>
> *Intercessors - Discover Your Prayer Power* (see endnotes) gives excellent details about each of the twelve types of anointing the Lord gives to intercessors. It lists a biblical example for each type, describing the strengths and zeals each type of anointing instills in an intercessor, and even noting pitfalls for each type and suggestions for how to avoid those pitfalls. In addition, the chapter on each intercessor type ends with a short list of five or six insightful questions, which can help intercessors discern which of the twelve types of anointing they have. *Intercessors - Discover Your Prayer Power* can be helpful to you, and is a powerful resource for those you enlist as intercessors.

Website articles

> Johnson, Nita (LaFond). "Melchizedek Priesthood." www.worldforjesus.org/articles-prophetic.php?ID=4.

DVDs/CDs

> Randy DeMain's sermons on the Sons of Issachar
> www.kingdomrevelation.org/product/sons-of-issachar

People

> Bruce Cook, Kingdom House Publishing, Kingdom Economic Yearly Summit (KEYS), and Glory Realm Ministries
> www.kingdomeconomicsummit.com
>
> Elizabeth Alves, Increase International
> www.increaseinternational.com About Us

Cathy Buettner, owner of Say It Well! Writing Services

Tommi Femrite, Gatekeepers International
www.gatekeepersintl.org

Billie Boatwright, Holy Ground International
www.holygroundinternational.org

Groups

Christian Business Network, Austin, TX | www.austincbn.org

International Christian Chamber of Commerce | www.iccc.net

Find, Engage, Release

"Our company has supplied equipment to contractors for more than ten years. In 2012, sales were $883,000. In 2013, sales were $1,554,000—a 76 percent increase. Why? How could we have done it again? We could not come up with anything that we or our staff had done that was responsible for more than a few percent. We had a meeting with our staff and came to the same conclusion—all of us start every day at the office by praying together. We have given the business to God, we are his shepherds, we love to give, and we partner with WISE Ministries. Charles and Liz Robinson give us ongoing personal prophecy and counseling. Their intercessory prayer team is indefatigable, and gives us written reports every two weeks on what God is saying as they pray for us. God takes good care of his own, and he gets all the glory!"

— EH, President

2

> *"I looked for someone among them who would build up the wall and stand before me in the gap on behalf of the land so I would not have to destroy it, but I found no one"* (Ezekiel 22:30).

As you engage professional level intercessors, they will function in many capacities; you'll have a team that applies spiritual intelligence to the work of the seven spheres of culture.

What Is Professional Level Intercession?

In this new career field called professional level intercession (named as such by apostle C. Peter Wagner), professional level intercessors (PLIs) are those trained in intercession. PLIs have a certain spiritual giftedness which allows them to see or hear in the Spirit, or both. They are good typists, good writers, good listeners, patient, and familiar with computer word processing software (so they can prepare intercession reports). These people usually have some secular skills, especially in business or via involvement in the seven mountains, such as video editing, teaching, business accounting, producing—any skillset or experienced background that would give them special insight or authority to pray. A pastor who wants to increase church income could minister to local businesses, and other enterprises, by offering the services of PLIs. PLIs can be on the church staff list in the same way that retired ministers or part-time counselors are. You get it, you name it. The PLI designation should be up there with CPC, CPA, DM, MBA, etc. The training and experience is no less rigorous, and

the spiritual warfare can get very interesting as well!

Your PLI(s), and other spiritual team members, will interface with you and (potentially) your other leaders and family members. He or she will create a spiritual climate in which you and your organization can have maximum protection from the enemy. You communicate with the Lord to identify the kingdom assignment(s) you have for your enterprise and family. The SAT will help you learn how to receive your assignment(s) from the Lord and communicate your message clearly to your target market. You will work with the direction the Lord gives you and your spiritual team, and follow it for your enterprise and personal daily life.

Helping leaders hear the voice of God better

WISE does not come in and tell you how you should run your enterprise or how to manage your employees. However, after trust is built, the consulting arm of what we do can get involved with personnel issues and strategic directional issues. WISE exists to help you better discern and know the voice of God for yourself. WISE becomes a sounding board for you to confirm that you really do hear the voice of the Lord—more than you may realize. The voice of God sounds like your thoughts, but there is a subtle spark of divine inspiration that WISE has which can help you learn to discern and detect. We have found that our leaders greatly increase in this ability to hear the voice of God since that is one of our main giftings.

> *"My sheep listen to my voice; I know them, and they follow me"* (John 10:27).

It's a privilege for all of God's people to hear his voice, but we all can hear more clearly as we exercise this gift. The job of WISE intercessors (and more for coaches) is to be your cheerleaders. They are there to encourage you to pursue the Lord's voice and to help build your faith. God wants to build a platform for your SAT to minister to you and your leaders from behind the scenes.

Why Pray?

Prayer is the single most powerful force for change in the universe. E.M. Bounds, a noted prayer warrior, said,[2]

> "Prayer is the greatest of all forces, because it honors God and brings Him into active aid."

He also stated,

> "Everything depends on prayer, and yet we neglect it not only to our own spiritual hurt but also to the delay and injury of our Lord's cause upon earth. The forces of good and evil are contending for the world. Had there been persistent, universal, and continuous prayer by God's people, long ago this the earth would have been possessed for Christ."

God allows us to partner with him in prayer to change situations. Someone may ask, "God is sovereign, so why do I need to pray?" The answer is that God *is* sovereign, but God, in his sovereignty, restricts himself to the limits of our partnership with him in prayer. God directs us, but we respond in prayers that bring heaven to earth. The will of God expressed through us, and the words spoken, bring to earth not only the will of God, but also *the manifestation of what we are praying about*—for us *and* you. How does intercession differ from prayer?

The differences between prayer and intercession

When you combine focused and targeted intercession (a higher form of prayer) for enterprises in all seven mountains of society, you can change any aspects or elements of society for good at their cores.

> **Prayer** is the act of obedience in bringing feelings and desires—words from our hearts—to life.
>
> **Intercession** denotes the carrying of a burden that is from God's heart.

We can pray about anything in our hearts, but to intercede means that we choose to stand in the gap for someone or something (e.g., a cause).

In intercession, we choose to become identified with that cause or individual. The intercessor carries a burden of the Lord which oftentimes is not released from him until that which he has been given to speak, and in some cases suffer, has been accomplished.[*][†]

---

[*] Intercessors can obviously be both men and women.
[†] See the table on page 17 which gives even more characteristics of the differences in prayer and intercession.

Our own Holy Spirit intercedes for us in sounds that cannot be uttered:

> *"In the same way, the Spirit helps us in our weakness. We do not know what we ought to pray for, but the Spirit himself intercedes for us through wordless groans"* (Rom. 8:26).

Jesus, himself, never ceases to make intercession for us at the right hand of the Father, as Scripture states in Romans 8:34:

> *"Who then is the one who condemns? No one. Christ Jesus who died—more than that, who was raised to life—is at the right hand of God and is also interceding for us."*

Opposition to the WISE model at a CEO round table group

I have been a part of a CEO round table group. Every month a member presents his or her business model, financial reports, challenges, etc. When it was my turn to present, a particular individual had a strong negative reaction due to the coupling of the words "professional" and "intercessor."

This individual said he was going to pray for the group on a regular basis, and more or less stated that we did not need a service that paid people to do it. I respected his comment and completed my presentation, after which several people said they were interested in the service.

The next month he mentioned to everyone that he was praying for us. We thanked him, but that was it—nothing more, no prayer requests, no follow up, nothing. That situation got me thinking—the level of prayer (and not even intercession) which the round table member practiced is the intercession paradigm which leaders have been used to and are conditioned to. Friend, we need to change this. I set it in my heart to respond formally with the following set of comparisons to show why the current paradigm is not enough.

Our company history illustrates that professional level intercession works. Think about our track record. How could WISE be in business since 2005 in this challenging economy (and our services are not cheap) if this service did not work? Not only have we been able to remain in business, this ministry has been our main source of full-time employment since 2005. When talking with Lance Wallnau, Lance stated that "many have tried this field and have not been

Prayer	Professional Level Intercession
I will pray for you if I remember	I will intercede for you at regular intervals
I maybe only know a general need	I will intercede for you according to knowledge of your life, family, and business(es)
I am a generalist	I am a specialist
I do not follow up with you	I follow up and ask for status updates regularly
I do not show you that I prayed	I produce a report for you on *what* I prayed
I speak to God; I do not ask him for specifics about you or your situation	I ask God what he has to say about the situation, then listen and record specifics he gives me about you and your situation
I may not pray for you for several weeks	I pray for you 2-3 times per week
I may be praying for old, answered requests. I do not followup with you to see if **the prayers were answered.**	I pray for only current, valid needs. I will follow up and will stop praying/pray for other issues when I am notified that **the prayers were answered**
You do not know what I am praying	You know *exactly* what I am praying since I write down my prayers for you
I cannot hear God speak clearly to me about you	I hear God speak to me every day about you and others, as I am gifted in this area
I pray in my spare time	I intercede in my *dedicated* time
I do not get paid for this	I get paid well and look forward to my time on your behalf
I pray for maybe 1-3 minutes for each need	I intercede for 30-60 minutes at a time
My prayers are limited to the one or two topics that you mentioned	My intercession is comprehensive; we put eight powerful prayer shields around you and your loved ones. We pray for important meetings, travel, spouse, children, other leaders, and your important business clients

This table lists characteristics of the current mindset about prayer compared to the characteristics of professional level intercession. The table illustrates how professional level intercession is at an entirely higher level than regular prayer, and carries with it the expectation of results.

successful in it, but you have; congratulations!" Our success is due to our model and calling.

The Lord often encourages us by having our clients acknowledge the powerful effects of our prayers. In one case, the intercession was so much a part of the increase that the leaders of the company got together and tried to reason how this increase had actually happened. The only deduction they could make was that it was because of the prayer! Yay God! (I must be careful to not take credit where credit is really due to the Lord; he is the one responsible, while the intercessors were his vessels.)

In the client's own words:

"Our business has just celebrated the receipt of over $100,000 for delivering four large commercial generators. We had paid for and housed these generators in our warehouse over a nine-month period. Our customer had given us a purchase order for the generators, but was then paralyzed by state bureaucrats, who insisted he could not install the generators without their permission. This dilemma was a subject for prayer for many months. Eventually we received permission to ship the generators, just before our fiscal year end, and this week the bill was paid in full! This is definitely a victory for all of us—WISE Ministries and our company."

> *"We are awed by the resolution of this most difficult situation."*

Review: sons of Issachar anointing

The sons of Issachar (I Chron. 12:32) knew the times and the seasons and what Israel was to do, when Israel was to do it, and who was anointed to do it. They were people of action who had revelation: they encamped on the Eastern (sunrise) Gate, were *servants* to their brothers in the other tribes, and were not looking for their own gain.

They have spiritual intelligence and are faithful, obedient servants whom God is raising up, and whom God can trust. They build others up rather than try to build up their own ministries. They have the heartbeat of God and the frequency of heaven. They love God; through obedience they are willing to fight to the death for the people to whom they are assigned.

Your Job

It is to find these anointed sons of Issachar and engage them, inform them, release them, and bless them; then watch the favor and breakthrough that happens in lives, families, and in all endeavors!

Jesus said "A servant is not greater than his master" (John 15:20). The job of your spiritual coaches and intercessors is not to tell you, the leaders in your enterprises, what to do. You are to partner with those who are in the Issachar tribe, who will act as a sounding board and help fine-tune your spiritual ears to hear God's voice.

Many are shifting gears in this season; are you shifting up or down? (If shifting down, remember the slingshot principles. The more you pull back, the farther you'll go, i.e., the more you rest and recharge, the further you'll go.) What is your organization's pace for this year?

God Needs Intercessors!

Ezekiel 22:30 says "I looked for someone among them who would build up the wall and stand before me in the gap on behalf of the land so I would not have to destroy it, but I found no one." This is an unfortunate and sad situation. God looked for someone to stand in for the *land* that he would not have to destroy it. He could find no one.

Godly leaders from all walks of life are exposed; the enemy has broken through the wall/hedge or, even worse, there was never any wall and God's people are being plundered by the enemy. People are going to hell, profits are being squandered, companies are going out of business, marriages are breaking, and children are being taken captive at the enemy's will, all because there is no hedge. There are no intercessors!

We and our faithful team members have dedicated our lives to protecting and empowering these precious ones so that the work of the enemy in their lives would cease, and that these leaders would fulfill their divine callings from God and reach a level of actualization and fulfillment they never would have known without the coaching, mentoring, and intercession WISE's team provided.

As your intercessors pray and intercede for you, they become the first line of defense for you, your business, and your family.

These are lifelong relationships God has sovereignly initiated. We, they, and God take what we do very seriously. God told me to make my leaders bulletproof. That is exactly what we do, through God's Holy Spirit. Leaders are taken through our novel coaching and mentoring  program of inner healing and discipleship (in the seven mountains). Their businesses are empowered to be as important to God as the local churches in their regions. Their enterprises become *outposts* for the kingdom of God in those territories with angels of war assigned to them. Their land becomes the *habitation* of angels, and their enterprises become *tools in the hand* of God for their regions, as well as for the people of their regions. Salvations occur when people walk into their businesses; people are knocked down by the power of God while walking into their establishments. Negotiations become much easier because of the presence of Holy Spirit. Favor falls and business expands effortlessly.

I remember we had one company double in size within twenty-four hours upon signing the contract; we had not even started praying! The blessing occurred because they had become *apostolically and prophetically aligned* with us.

We have paid a great price to get to where we are, to become Josephs. Remember in Ps. 105:17 "the word of the Lord tested Joseph." That great price is all worth it to birth sons and daughters in the kingdom.

In many of our companies, we experience more of the power of God than we do in our churches. I am not putting down the church. Jesus loves his bride, the church, but the warfare in the marketplace is greater than the warfare in the church, so we need more of God's power there.

Back to the passage: there is no one to stand in the gap, to make a hedge or wall—a first line of defense against the *wiles,* attacks, and deception of the devil. Eph. 6:11 tells us to take on the full armor of God to resist the devil's plans. Leaders of all types need to be taught *how* to stand (the purpose of our God's Generals Certification Course).

As your intercessors pray and intercede for you, they become the first line of defense for you, your business, and your family. The enemy is going to have to go through *them* to get to you. (Comforting, is it not?) That is why you must be strong in the Lord, know him, and be experienced in spiritual warfare. There is no room for novices here. Your WISE team has the experience and the knowledge to build your strategic prayer shield. Our intercession has been proven over time in all seven mountains.

> *Perhaps you identify more with being a coach, but every coach needs to be an intercessor at some level, because coaches always will pray for their clients, just not for hours per day, as may be the case for intercessors. Coaches usually pray for their clients during the coaching session.*

Doors Unlocked for YOU

Many of you reading have had profound promises from the Lord. The relationship between king and prophet, if you will, can produce the things the Lord has promised you, and you can see those great and mighty prophetic words fulfilled through the relationships that are established between you and your spiritual advisory team. In many cases, these are lifelong journeys that the two of you will travel on together. Can you see this? Can you believe this? If you can *see* it, you can *have* it. This career and this training is the manifestation or the *key* to what God has been promising you all these years, and the precious fruit of these God-ordained relationships will last forever!‡

Convergence

When all the life lessons, tests, wisdom gained, and cumulative experiences come together to empower you for the main assignment of your life, you reach convergence.

You will enter convergence, and your spiritual advisory team will empower you and your leaders to be in convergence as well.

> *"Do you know that only 20 percent of leaders in the body of Christ ever enter into convergence in the work that God has called them to do? Being in convergence is the secret to getting to the top of anything."*
> — Dr. Lance Wallnau, The Seven Mountain Strategy

---

‡ See the text on page 71 called "Destiny Links," a term coined by Sandie Freed, for more discussion on the relationship aspect of this ministry.

Module 2: Endnotes

1. WISE Ministries. "Services." www.coachmybusiness.com/services-main.php
2. Bounds, E.M. *Classic Collection on Prayer.* Sydney: ReadHowYouWant, 2011.
3. WISE Ministries. "Intercession for Christian Leaders." www.coachmybusiness.com/Intercession_for_Christian_Leaders_2.pdf (accessed June 4, 2014).

Recommended Additional Resources for Leaders

Books

> Hillman, Os. *The 9 To 5 Window: How Faith Can Transform the Workplace*
>
> Hamon, Bill. *Prophetic Scriptures Yet to Be Fulfilled: During the 3rd and Final Reformation*
>
> Wagner, C. Peter. *Prayer Shield: How to Intercede for Pastors, Christian Leaders and Others on the Spiritual Frontlines* Prayer Warrior Series (Book 2)
>
> Alves, Beth, Tommi Femrite, and Karen Kaufmann. *Intercessors - Discover Your Prayer Power.*
>
> Freed, Sandie. *Destiny Thieves: Defeat Seducing Spirits and Achieve Your Purpose in God*

Website articles

> Wallnau, Lance. "How to Crack the Code that Unlocks You." www.lancelearning.biz/crack-the-code.

DVDs/CDs

> Randy DeMain's sermons on the Sons of Issachar www.kingdomrevelation.org
>
> Lance Wallnau, "Take All 7" 4 DVD series www.lancelearning.com
>
> Os Hillman, Lance Wallnau, and others "7 Mountain Strategies: Keys for Cultural Influence" Audio CD Series, www.7culturalmountains.org

People

> Lance Wallnau | www.lancewallnau.com
>
> Sandie Freed | www.sandiefreed.com

Executive Coaching

"Charles, you gave me a word that a credit was coming to me from a lawyer. Out of the blue, a lawyer contacted me two weeks later with a surprise credit that was due to my wife from over two years ago. It was enough to cover our rent that was due in days. Praise God."

— SHC, Calgary, AB

"I could have saved myself a lot of misery over the years by watching out for those who had my back. I more than ever realize the importance of certain intercessors in certain places. I understand that having the wrong people praying for you can hinder the things God wants to do in your life. Many of these things I learned the hard way, so take Charles's information to heart and save yourself a lot of distress, financial losses, as well as setbacks that could probably have been avoided by properly surrounding yourself with a strong hedge of defenses."

— Bill Smith
CEO, Now Enterprises, Inc.

3

"I have told you these things, so that in me you may have peace. In this world you will have trouble. But take heart! I have overcome the world" (John 16:33).

"The prayer of a righteous person is powerful and effective" (James 5:16b).

Going From Intercession to Intervention

As a leader in the seven mountains, you want your spiritual destiny to be clear to both you and the world. Is the destiny of your enterprise being interfered with, distorted, or cancelled out; or is it getting through with clarity and consistency and being reinforced?

The enemy will try to confuse or distort your message, possibly through miscommunication, or by combining some of the world's philosophies and/or your own personal misperceptions, leading you to give a mixed message through your enterprise.

> *Your PLI and spiritual coach can help run interference on the enemy's interference, thus neutralizing his effect on you and your enterprise.*

Often, the spiritual intelligence we need requires that we go from plain intercession (reactive) to intervention by running interference (proactive). We do it in the same way that football offensive fullbacks and tight ends run ahead of a halfback as he carries the ball and blocks prospective tacklers out of the way. It could also be compared to the way your defensive players run interference for your teammates if one of them takes possession of the ball when your team is on defense. Interference can also mean the act of illegally hindering an opponent from catching a forward pass or a kick.

Your intercessors are going ahead of you in the Spirit and blocking the enemy so you can move forward.

When you run interference, you stop being passive and become active in clearing the airwaves. Your PLIs run interference on the enemy. Say this out loud:

"I run interference on the enemy."

You have a message to receive from God. Your potential business clients have a message to receive from you. It's simple: clear up the communication channels to enhance your message!

Interference also pertains to linguistics. If there is a lot of babbling in your industry, how can you stand apart? The enemy may be trying to confuse or distort your message. Is your message getting out or is there overlap and miscommunication?

Let's ensure maximum clarity on both ends and hire informed, professional level intercessors and spiritual coaches to teach you how to communicate your message well.

Your enterprise is a tool of heaven to bring transformation to your region and sphere of influence, and it is specifically that destiny that Satan will try to block.

Your intercessors and spiritual coaches recognize that all who are working for the advancement of God's kingdom come into spiritual opposition from God's enemy—the Devil and his minions. The enemy's goal is to oppose the truth of God, which often takes the form of distorting the truth. The enemy would like you and your SAT team to have difficulty receiving the clear messages of God for their assignment.

Three steps for a PLI to bring clarity to your message

You can have a full release of your divine purpose if you, as the leader, have a clear channel of communication to God. It produces clarity; it allows the message of your products or services to convey your enterprise's spiritual destiny to your intended audience (there is no weakening, distortion, or cancelation—think of a bad radio signal). Your PLI and coach or chief revelatory officer (CRO) can use a three-prong strategy to approach this.

1. Use intercession (intervention) to "clear the airwaves" over your enterprise.
2. Go from a passive role to an active role (interference).
3. Use coaching to develop your personal spirit and habits to be more in tune with God through the Word, inner healing of emotional issues, and self-defeating behavior, and the infilling of the Spirit of God.

Helping you hear and communicate the truth of your enterprise's spiritual destiny is an important part of the professional level intercession you receive.

Placing a Hedge/Prayer Shield Around You and Your Family

Your intercessors seek to place a hedge of protection around those for whom they pray. In Job 1:10 Satan says, "Have you not put a hedge around him and his household and everything he has? You have blessed the work of his hands, so that his flocks and herds are spread throughout the land."

Satan was affected by God's hedge of protection; his reach was limited because of the hedge that was placed around Job. Satan was like a junkyard dog on a leash; he could bark and growl at Job and threaten to charge, but only when God allowed it could he touch Job. In all cases he was not allowed to kill Job.

From this example, we know that the principle of a spiritual hedge works. This is what we seek to establish when we pray. In fact, there are eight powerful prayer shields or hedges that we build around you and your family, leaders, and even your customers.

> *Marital*
>
> *Safety/protection*
>
> *Travel schedule/major meetings/presentations*
>
> *Sexual/moral/ethical*
>
> *Physical health and well-being*
>
> *Family*
>
> *Personal/financial*
>
> *Business/ministry*

How to Set Up Prayer Shields

Your PLI will construct and maintain prayer shields both for you and for your customers. As the book *Intercessors - Discover Your Prayer Power* says, there are pros and cons for constructing prayer shields, and the cons are not good reasons to not set them up. As you will see us say elsewhere in this text: leaders *need* intercessors![2]

Reasons to have prayer shields

Leaders *need* intercessors. Get the spiritual protection you need for breakthrough to the next level without all the attacks from the enemy. Let your intercessors do your fighting for you so you have the time and energy to hear from God on how to lead more effectively. Don't forget to pray for your intercessors also. Intercessors protect you from enemy attack and/or distractions and confirm what God is telling you.

An intercessor is a person to whom you give permission to speak into your life. When she has permission to speak into your life, God will tell her intimate things about you. Don't have spiritual arrogance; you need intercessors to help you recognize your blind spots. *Choose* intercessors you know personally, so you know their strengths and weaknesses. You don't tell all your struggles to all levels of intercessors. If you travel with your ministry, it is especially important to choose intercessors in different time zones. Hold yourself accountable to your intercessors; God is not into lone rangers.

As your authority increases, so do the attacks against you (sometimes through temptations like greed, power, pride, gluttony, alcohol, sex, and drugs; other times through the release of curses against your call, foundational teachings, fruit, marriage, health, and seed) to get your focus off what you're called to do.

If you have a business and/or ministry, you need a shield for them, as well as a personal shield for yourself. The shield size increases as the number of your employees increases.[3] You don't need a huge number of intercessors; you just need the *right* ones.

Knowing who you are in Christ—knowing your identity—unlocks your destiny.

Reasons some people do NOT have intercessors:
- They are rough, tough loners who say they don't need them. (These people are leaving themselves, their families, and finances open to attack.)
- They are uninformed and don't know about the need.
- They think they don't need prayer if they go to church; however, the reverse is true—if they go to church, they are on Satan's hit list, and need prayer!
- They know they need prayer but are naïve about how important being covered with intercessory prayer is. If they don't understand the need, then they don't understand the importance of their callings.

How do you develop your prayer shield?

List people you know or think are praying for you now. Then ask. Most people are willing to surround you in prayer.

Possible Intercessors (Follow up later!)
1)
2)
3)
4)
5)
6)
7)

An intercessor should:
1. Be an honorable person, a person of integrity whose yes is yes and no is no, who means what she says and says what she means, who is the same person in all areas of her life, lives by the word of God, and carries Jesus Christ with her wherever she goes rather than letting her "flesh hang out."
2. Be able to keep confidentiality, a person who doesn't even share a prayer request with another for the purpose of that person joining him in prayer. If your intercessor violates your confidentiality, write him a letter thanking him for serving you, but releasing him from your intercessor list. Also confront him personally about the specific issue of confidentiality you know has been violated (as per Matthew 18).
3. Be able to listen to God (she is quiet and knows how to hear his voice).
4. Understand authority and walk in it. He is confident, knows how to stand in the authority his anointing gives him, and prays boldly.
5. Be teachable and trainable. She goes to meetings where people teach about intercession; she doesn't think she knows it all, even if she is equipped.
6. Be committed to pray for you (when God speaks to him to pray for you, he knows when to pray and when to respond.)
7. Have a call from God to pray for you, your ministry/business, or any endeavor. God spoke to her heart to have an anointing to pray for you as an individual.
8. Be humble (agree with what God says about him, "I am an intercessor; my anointing is ____; God speaks to me).
9. Be willing to stand firm in the gap for you.
10. Be able to share with you in a way that is not intimidating, and present information she has heard from God in a palatable way.
11. Be humble (agree with what God says about him, "I am an intercessor; my anointing is; God speaks to me).
12. Be willing to stand firmly in the gap for you.
13. Be able to share with you in a way that is not intimidating, and present information she has heard from God in a palatable way.

Your Responsibility as a Leader and Some More Terms

CEOs need to take responsibility for the spiritual health of their companies and employees. The CEO is not only the chief executive, but also the chief spiritual officer (CSO). WISE does not come in as the CSO. In the capacity that I, Charles, operate in, WISE comes alongside as the chief revelatory officer (CRO).

The purpose of the CRO or spiritual coach is to be a single point of contact between the C-level people and the board at the client's enterprise, and the intercessors. The CRO is to be a filter for the large amount of revelation that is given by the Lord such as dreams, visions, prophetic words, discernment, senses, warnings, etc. Without a single leader—someone with a gift of wisdom, someone who is very mature in the Lord, and is able to filter potentially conflicting and confusing information, chaos could ensue. For example, not everyone who prophesies is a prophet and everyone, even prophets, can sometimes miss the mark in their ministry. We see through a glass darkly and know in part: "For now we see only a reflection as in a mirror; then we shall see face to face. Now I know in part; then I shall know fully, even as I am fully known" (I Cor. 13:12). That is why we all need each other, and we need the gift of wisdom in operation in the CRO function:

> "To one there is given through the Spirit a message of wisdom, to another a message of knowledge by means of the same Spirit, to another faith by the same Spirit, to another gifts of healing by that one Spirit, to another miraculous powers, to another prophecy, to another distinguishing between spirits, to another speaking in different kinds of tongues, and to still another the interpretation of tongues. All these are the work of one and the same Spirit, and he distributes them to each one, just as he determines" (I Cor. 12:8-11).

Leaders, do not bypass the SAT when it comes to hiring or moving people into key positions. God must be consulted first so that your business decisions remain in his will. If you don't, you cannot expect the intercessors to pray and move God's hand on behalf of these decisions, and you can't blame your poor decisions on them either.

Ask God *and* consult your SAT for confirmation. WISE is in your life to be a godly sounding board and to provide that word of endorsement.

What is Life Coaching?

Life coaching is all about helping people get from where they are, in their lives, to where they want to be. If we are all honest with ourselves, we know we could do with improving an area or two of our lives. We *know* what to do to become more successful, but we don't do what we know. Life coaches help bridge the gap between where you are and where you want to be.

It is a life coach's job to help people get what they want in life in by breaking down the barriers that they impose on themselves. WISE combines traditional coaching with counseling to produce a hybrid model that has proven very effective. Christian life coaches serve their clients through the love of Jesus Christ in a faith-based, biblical approach.

The Role of a WISE Certified 7M Spiritual, Life, or Executive Coach

Rather than actually *telling* you the answers, a WISE 7M CPC is the catalyst for helping you find the answers yourself. By asking challenging and thought-provoking questions, a coach can unlock your potential.

Coaching is forward looking and focused on the action you are willing to take to get what you want out of life.

Sometimes you just can't see the forest through the trees. You are so wrapped up in everyday life that it just passes you by! Coaching enables you to take a step back and actually examine your life and *all* of its components (not forgetting the spiritual components). This leads to greater self-awareness, focus, and accountability.

A faith-based life coach is

- your personal life trainer to enable you to achieve your goals,
- your champion and cheerleader during a turnaround and transition,
- your trainer in communication and life skills,
- your sounding board when making important choices,
- your motivator when strong actions are called for,
- your unconditional support when you take a hit,
- your mentor in personal self-development,
- your co-designer when creating an extraordinary project,
- your beacon and friend during stormy times,

- your wake-up call if you don't hear your own.
- your partner in helping you have all of what matters most to you.

How does coaching work?

Spiritual, life, and executive coaching can be done in person, on the telephone, or using e-mail. Group coaching can be done in person or over the phone (tele-class). WISE will coach you one-on-one.

During each coaching session, you and your coach will discuss and explore your journey. We'll include your goals, wins, challenges, frustrations, and opportunities, as well as develop fieldwork for the coming week.

Fieldwork isn't like the homework you were assigned in school—it consists of action steps to move you closer toward the realization of your goals and dreams. You bring the agenda and the coach brings the coaching skills to create a partnership that moves you forward, all in the framework of 7M marketplace ministry.

You and your coach (SC) schedule coaching sessions that are usually biweekly and last from a half hour to an hour. Sessions may be focused on one specific goal or challenge, or on a much broader set of personal or professional issues. Your life can be powerfully changed through Christian life coaching.

Module 3: Endnotes

1. Servello, PR Mike. *God's Shield of Protection*. Holland Patent: DS Lisi, 2003.

2. Alves, Beth, Tommi Femrite, and Karen Kaufmann. *Intercessors - Discover Your Prayer Power*. Ventura: Regal, 2000. [Much on the topic of prayers shields is covered in this book. The book instructs how to gather and recruit intercessors for prayer shields, how to determine which intercessor types to use in different prayer shields, and what characteristics qualify/disqualify intercessors. In addition, it gives recommendations for how to set up a regular schedule of communications, how to regularly evaluate your shields, and how or why to release an intercessor.]

3. Cook, Dr. Bruce. "Spiritual Due Diligence™." www.kingdomventures.com/pdf/SpiritualDueDiligence.pdf

4. Wagner, C. Peter. *Prayer Shield: How to Intercede for Pastors, Christian Leaders and Others on the Spiritual Frontlines* Prayer Warrior series (Book 2). Ventura: Regal, 1994.

Sources and Additional Resources for Leaders

Books

> Hillman, Os. *The 9 to 5 Window: How Faith Can Transform the Workplace*
>
> Cook, Dr. Bruce. *Aligning With The Apostolic, Volume 1: Apostles And The Apostolic Movement In The Seven Mountains Of Culture*
>
> Hamon, Bill. *The Day of the Saints: Equipping Believers for Their Revolutionary Role in Ministry*

People

> Tony Stolzfus, Leadership Metaformation | www.meta-formation.com

Groups

> Christian Business Network, Austin, TX | www.cbnaustin.org

Favor & Breakthrough

"As the founder and CEO of a company that reaches directly into all seven mountains of culture, including nearly half of all Fortune 100 corporations, our partnership with WISE Ministries has been invaluable. We would not be as effective, nor have the influence that we do, without its support and friendship."

— Randy S., Washington State

"Charles and Liz Robinson of WISE have the knowledge, the heart, and the experience to provide intercessors for business. Because of our excellent experiences as their clients, I hope the Robinsons continue to disciple many more intercessors. We know firsthand how gifted the Robinsons are, since, from 2005, we have both watched them shepherd their employees, and benefited from their guidance for us as we steered our business through many adventures.

Simply said, Charles and Liz Robinson were given to us by God, who knew that we needed the friendship, mentoring, and spiritual authority they possess to move forward in his purposes—not only in our business life but also in our personal walks with him. They are the real deal, and operate in the true anointing of Father because of the level of intimacy they each keep with him. They are our friends, comrades-in-arms in spiritual warfare, and our spiritual mentors all in one!"

— Reverend Dorinda Trick
counselor

4

"And see if I will not throw open the floodgates of heaven and pour out so much blessing that there will not be room enough to store it" (Malachi 3:10).

The Joseph Experience

God is raising up many leaders in the field of marketplace ministry through "Joseph" experiences. Os Hillman has written much about this phenomenon, in which the Lord takes a Christian in the seven mountains through a difficult time of testing. The Christian leader may lose most or all material possessions and/or relationships in the process of refining her total dependence on God. In the process, the "Joseph" Christians may also go through several tests to see if their character is mature enough for the leadership positions the Lord is preparing them to have in the coming moves of God in the seven mountains.

Why is the marketplace such a critical area for ministry? Rich Marshall, author of *God@Work* and *God@Work2*,[1] feels the Scripture has been fulfilled in the Bible verse Luke 10:2: "The harvest is plentiful, but the workers are few. Ask the Lord of the harvest, therefore, to send out workers into his harvest field." Rich relates how, in the United States as well as other countries, more workers are not Christian than are Christian. However, Christians from many different denominations (the workers) are spread throughout the workforce among the unbelievers (the harvest fields). Those workers have learned how to work together in their jobs; implementing them to work together for kingdom purposes is just the next step we need to accomplish for the sake of what God has planned for the seven mountains.

Cities of Gold

While going through a SOZO inner healing session,* Holy Spirit told me that he wanted to take me to meet someone. He led me to a sea of hot coals. I could see Jesus in the distance. Jesus said I was to walk across the hot coals and to take my shoes off before walking. I said "I cannot, Lord, it will burn me!" Jesus assured me that I could do it. I took my shoes off and walked across.

Next, I came upon a river of fire. Jesus was very close now, but there was no way I could go through that river; Jesus knew this was too much for me, so he stood up on his throne and reached out. (His arms became extremely long; he lifted me up over the river of fire and plopped me right on his lap!) Jesus then showed me a dark city. He threw a handful of gold and the city lit up with an amazing show of light, color, and splendor. Then he repeated the same action over another city, then another. He spoke to me and said, "Charles, I have called you as a Joseph to the sheep nations and cities." The vision ceased.

I had to go through the river of fire to reach that point. "They strengthened the disciples in these cities and encouraged the disciples to remain faithful. Paul and Barnabas told them, 'We must suffer a lot to enter the kingdom of God'" (Acts 14:22 GWT).

The visions all unite to explain Josephs together forming a patchwork

Several months after the cities of gold experience, I was sitting in my office when I "saw" myself at an ironing board. I was ironing a nondescript fragment of cloth that was incomplete by itself; it had a definite color (green) and a definite texture. It was thick, appearing to be made of a heavenly substance I could not identify. It was almost as if the piece of cloth were my own life and I was processing it … ironing out the wrinkles. I was feeling alone, feeling I was not making much of an impact. The vision expanded: I saw many other Josephs ironing out the fabric of their lives, ironing out the wrinkles in circumstances and relationships, seemingly feeling alone and in obscurity. Next, I saw a most amazing mantle, a garment, if you will. Each piece of fabric was now sewn into each of the other pieces. Even though there were numerous colors and countless types of fabrics and textures, each piece fit together into the garment perfectly.

---

* SOZO is the Greek word translated "saved, healed, delivered." Sozo ministry is a unique inner healing and deliverance ministry aimed to get to the root of things hindering your personal connection with the Father, Son, and Holy Spirit.

These individual pieces were not symmetrical, but all shapes and sizes, yet, when they were fitted together, not one piece overlapped the boundaries of another and there was not one gap in the garment. It was splendid! There was no lack; everything had been provided for by God and his Josephs—solutions, inventions, creativity, provision, protection—and the mantle covered it all! I discovered that this, the fabric of our lives, was Joseph's coat of many colors which will be worn by all of the Josephs, universally, in this final hour.

I subsequently did some research on Joseph's coat and learned that one reference[4] said it was a patchwork quilt.

This became the theme of our Tipping Point Unconference in 2013—the coat and a new anointing for that patchwork quilt. The patchwork quilt is what God is birthing through us—his Josephs and the intercessors and coaches who support the Josephs. (Note that the intercessors and coaches who support the Josephs shall themselves also become Josephs.) The patchwork quilt provides all that is needed.

There is a new wisdom and a new anointing for the times in which we live. Daniel 12:3 states that in the latter days "those who are wise will shine like the brightness of the heavens, and those who lead many to righteousness, like the stars for ever and ever." You are called to shine in this new career field which you have chosen. Many will come to the Lord's light. This wisdom is called the Daniel or Joseph anointing. We as PLIs are called to turn many to righteousness— God's righteousness and character and integrity. *He will shine* through us in the midst of a very great darkness (see Is. 61), and we will reflect his glory as the moon reflects the light of the sun at night. In the way that Joseph had the answers when Pharaoh asked him for the interpretation of his dream,[†] we will have the answers, the interpretations, when the questions are asked. The problems which will face us are of an order of magnitude greater than any problems that have faced us previously.

---

† Of the seven fat cows and the seven skinny cows that ate the fat cows (see Gen. 37-50)

Spiritual Gates

We will also have the *solutions*—great and ingenious ones. We will have heavenly solutions which will have come down from heaven through us. The number of solutions and inventions will have greater impact than those which came before. Angels reserved from the foundation of the world, who have never been released, will be released. We will operate as a modern-day Jacob's ladder which stretches to heaven—one upon which the angels ascend and descend. Most importantly, the Lord is at the top of the ladder directing the angelic activity (even over your life).

> Jacob ... had a dream in which he saw a stairway resting on the earth, with its top reaching to heaven, and the angels of God were ascending and descending on it. There above it stood the Lord ... When Jacob awoke from his sleep, he thought, "Surely the Lord is in this place, and I was not aware of it." He was afraid and said, "How awesome is this place! This is none other than the house of God; this is the gate of heaven" (Gen. 28:10-17).

Jacob named that place Bethel, which means "house of God." He redefined the purpose of that place.

Warfare to open and close gates

God uses WISE Ministries to open portals (or gates, if you will) and to displace forces of darkness over enterprises, cities, regions, and territories. Gates are very strategic.

The enemy understands this as well. Warfare is ongoing in the seven mountains, more heavily in some mountains than in others. Ruling spirits fight to open and close gates of access. Opening a gate allows unhampered heavenly access to an area, while closing a gate restricts access by malevolent spirits. An important detail to recall about gates is that the city gates were where financial transactions occurred in the city. The arts & entertainment mountain is an area where we definitely see warfare at the present time. New age leaders understand the importance of gates in their respective regions and areas of influence. WISE regularly addresses and counters the New Age takeover of Hollywood, such as the time I opened a gate through prayer in downtown Hollywood above the Walk of the Stars during Halloween, 2011.

Gates in the Bible

Psalm 24:7-9 is all about gates: "Lift up your heads, you gates; be lifted up, you ancient doors, that the King of glory may come in. Who is this King of glory? The Lord strong and mighty, the Lord mighty in battle. Lift up your heads, you gates; lift them up, you ancient doors, that the King of glory may come in."

Your intercessors and spiritual coaches are gate openers and territory definers.

Warfare can be at the level of principalities; remember that both fallen angels and God's angels are considered principalities.

God has his principalities, his archangels. Your enterprise can have strong, even arch-angels assigned to it. It also can have evil principalities operating through it because of iniquity in, or curses on, the people in those organizations, regions, or territories. We are to open heavenly portals (open heaven) of revelation over our organizations so that the angels have access when needed, and so they can bring the resources "down the ladder" from heaven. By the way, you are the ladder they descend through!

In Matthew 18:16, Jesus says for every fact to be confirmed by two or three witnesses: "But if they will not listen, take one or two others along, so that 'every matter may be established by the testimony of two or three witnesses.'" I Cor. 14:3 tells us that prophecy is given for edification, exhortation, and comfort. "But the one who prophesies speaks to people for their strengthening, encouraging and comfort."

"It is the Spirit of prophecy who bears testimony to Jesus" (Rev. 19:10b), so prophecy is the voice of Jesus. The Spirit of prophecy builds up, encourages, confirms, and brings comfort and rousing calls to change. In contrast, someone who is operating in the office of the prophet may say words that are not so comforting to people, such as words of correction, which are for their good: "And He gave some *as* apostles, and some *as* prophets, and some *as* evangelists, and some *as* pastors and teachers, *for the equipping of the saints for the work of service*, to the building up of the body of Christ … but speaking the truth in *love*, we are to grow up in *all aspects* into Him who is the head, *even* Christ" (Eph. 4:11-12,15 NASB, emphasis mine). The office of the prophet is the office of one operating in a much higher level of anointing of prophecy and revelation than is seen in someone who has a prophetic mantle or someone who is operating in the simple gift of prophecy.

> *Your intercessors and coaches are gate openers and territory definers.*

The purpose of this course is not to delve into the depths of the theology of the prophetic, but rather to emphasize that this gift is essential for ministering to you, and it is used to discern the real battle going on in your life and organization. It is advantageous for the PLI to flow in the realm of prophecy.‡ There are many good books on the prophetic. I recommend Dr. Bill Hamon's excellent book *Prophets and Personal Prophecy: God's Prophetic Voice Today*.

A New Finishing Anointing—Josephs Work Together

We are running in a finishing *new anointing* now. You see, Joseph was a planner—not just a dreamer, not just an interpreter. He was strategic and methodical. He personally supervised the building of the storage containers so that when the famine struck, the grain was ready to fulfill the needs of the people. That supply lasted for seven years (see Gen. 41). God is doing the same thing today and many lives shall be saved, even unbelievers', through God's *new Josephs*, of which you are a part. You must be, for how can you interpret the mysteries and the dreams of your business team and bring them into breakthrough unless you have a new Joseph anointing?

This is also combined with the Issachar anointing.

---

‡ See my comments about baptism in Holy Spirit on page 81.

Favor and breakthrough — you can have them in your own life and in the lives of your clients.

Favor

If there were any areas where I could say specifically that WISE has an anointing or ability, it would be in the areas of favor and breakthrough. I would define *favor* as seeing doors open without your having to do anything in the natural realm to cause them to open. For example, rather than favor simply showing up in the form of phone calls for orders on a new product—a product we had just advertised on the *Home Shopping Network*—favor would be the president of HSN saying, "Not only do we like the one product, but we want to add your *entire line* to our upcoming shows!" Now *that* is favor.

God's favor comes out of the blue and hits you like a ton of bricks, in a good way. God's favor floors you and leaves you speechless. God's favor does not come from nothing—you either have the fruit of favor in your life (which is produced from obedience and sacrifice), or you partner with someone who has it, and voilà, things change almost immediately.

For example, when someone brings WISE on board, logjams in the spirit realm become dislodged. I can't tell how many people have said that as soon as we began to pray for them, they felt something shift. Something does shift; it's like God takes the favor which is on our lives and places it on your enterprise. Not only that, but he *loves* to do it! Do I sound excited about the subject of favor, God's divine favor, heaven's favor? It's because *I am*.

We at WISE have paid the price for this, although I will not go into all the reasons why. You have this course in your hands, and you will benefit from this favor as well. May it be imparted to you through the reading of this manual. We are nothing special in ourselves, but he calls us special and beloved. He is the only one who is begotten of the Father and worthy of all praise, because Jesus paid the price so that we could walk in the Father's favor.

Breakthrough

Breakthrough is a spiritual force, and it may even be an angel. Breakthrough is that supernatural power that overcomes an obstacle. It is very closely tied to the gift of faith—not just saving faith, but supernatural faith which can do the miraculous (see I Cor:12). Breakthrough comes in many different forms, but some of the more common ways are through praise and worship. Ascending to such a level in warfare praise breaks through the enemy's hold over your mind, body, emotions, etc.; or someone else's mind, body, or emotions.

Breakthrough may come into a situation or circumstance by bringing a divine healing, a sudden order that was needed, or an unexpected payment.

Whatever the area of breakthrough needed, angels are certainly involved as well.

Perhaps the angel Gabriel is involved in delivering an important piece of communication you have been waiting for, or the angel Michael is involved in defeating the enemy that has been oppressing you (or perhaps a lesser angel), is involved in the breakthrough. How God does it is immaterial, but the fact that he does it is the point. The fact that one minute ago something happened and I, or my situation, or my wife's situation is not the same anymore, means that a miracle happened. This is what WISE Ministries brings to the table. Things change when we come aboard; we feel the warfare immediately and go into battle, many times against a ruling spirit that is involved, and God breaks it. God's favor floors you and leaves you speechless.

We are not novices; we have been involved in many battles with territorial spirits, spirits the Bible calls rulers in high places. "For our struggle is not against flesh and blood, but against the rulers, against the authorities, against the powers of this dark world and against the spiritual forces of evil in the heavenly realms" (Eph. 6:12).

Many times the battle is totally invisible and does not manifest in the natural; however, sometimes it manifests in the natural with signs and wonders.

Expect breakthrough as a WISE client. You may desperately need breakthrough, although you most likely could not put it into words. Breakthrough comes through Holy Spirit administrating or directing the angels, on the behalf of another toward you, through their words and bodies. They are conduits for his flowing power and administration. Their words are eternal and powerful and divinely inspired as they direct the flow of the river of God to bring that needed breakthrough to the earth realm from the heavenly realm. God even wants to do these things through you.

Experience his love and his breakthrough and his favor right now. Enjoy it, bask in it. You are going to a new level right now; by faith claim it and receive it. Receive a new anointing!

Module 4: Endnotes

1. Marshall, Rich. *God@Work* and *God @ Work: Developing Ministers in the Marketplace*, Vol. 2. Shippensburg: Destiny Image Publishers, 2005.

2. Myers, Erin. "Patchwork Quilting —A History Summary" Fibre2Fashion. www.fibre2fashion.com/industry-article/business- management-articles-reports/patchwork-quilting-a-history-summary/ patchwork-quilting-a-history-summary1.asp

3. Hamon, Bill, and Oral Roberts. *Prophets and Personal Prophecy: God's Prophetic Voice Today*. Shippensburg: Destiny Image, 2011. Cook, Dr. Bruce. *Partnering With The Prophetic: Portfolios, Protocols, Patterns & Processes.* Lakebay: Kingdom House Publishing, 2011.

Recommended Additional Resources for Leaders

Books

Hillman, Os. *The 9-5 Window: How Faith Can Transform the Workplace*

DVDs/CDs/MP3s

Hillman, Os. "How We Lost the 7 Mountains" MP3, www.tgifbookstore.com

People

Rich Marshall, ROI | godisworking.com

C. Peter Wagner, Wagner Leadership Institute
www.wagnerleadership.org

Spiritual Services

"I have been using the services of WISE Ministries for the last three months and have found it to be a tremendous blessing. The team has been very supportive of me, and my coach was great. She always had an encouraging word to say and many words of wisdom.

The prayers and support I received really helped me, and I know that the Lord was answering those prayers and healing me of various issues and challenges I was facing. It was great to know that I had a team of committed people supporting me through some very difficult times.

I wouldn't hesitate to recommend WISE to anyone."

— Natalie B., Darby, England

5

"Now to the one who works, wages are not credited as a gift but as an obligation" (Romans 4:4).

"The worker deserves his wages" (Luke 10:7b).

Your Spiritual Advisory Team Is Paid to Solve Problems

The ultimate breakthroughs all belong to God. Your SAT moves in his power, his revelation, and his grace. Jesus said "I no longer call you servants, because a servant does not know his master's business. Instead, I have called you friends, for everything that I learned from my Father I have made known to you" (John 15:5). God will make you look good through your SAT. Remember that. You look good when you simply work alongside your SAT and are obedient in relating and, in some cases interpreting, revelation.

Obedience is the currency of heaven. Jesus said, "If you love me, keep my commands" (John 14:15). Obedience is equivalent to love in the Bible. If you are obedient, you will be successful in solving problems for your organization. Solving problems entails getting to the root of those problems. There are many different types of problems which need solving—financial, marital, personnel, operational—or controlling spirits, confusion in the marketing and message, etc. Sometimes the problems have to do with the leadership

and those whom you have hired. As I said before, your allegiance must be to the Lord, who is your ultimate source. He will help you to urge and coax you, in love, to change.

> "Therefore, I urge you, brothers and sisters, in view of God's mercy, to offer your bodies as a living sacrifice, holy and pleasing to God—this is your true and proper worship. Do not conform to the pattern of this world, but be transformed by the renewing of your mind. Then you will be able to test and approve what God's will is—his good, pleasing and perfect will" (Rom. 12:1-2).

He has called you to your line of work. "Being confident of this, that he who began a good work in you will carry it on to completion until the day of Christ Jesus" (Phil. 1:6).

> *You, as the leader, are the chief spiritual officer (CSO), and you have the ultimate say (and responsibility) when dealing with the spiritual matters of your organization. I urge you to decicate or rededicate your organization to the Lord, even right now. The Lord Jesus is the CEO, but you are also the CEO—Christ's Equipped Officer.*

You Charge for Prayer? New Times Demand New Methods

I need to rephrase the question. You charge for the intercessor's time? The answer is YES. The prayer is offered up freely, but the time is not. In other words, the time of the intercessor is valuable and, as such, he should be compensated for the time spent in lifting up your various needs. Of course we charge for coaching.

We want to validate and verify the need for certification in the intercession and coaching fields—both for professionalism and accountability. [Currently coaching is an unregulated field. There are many types of coaching and coaches (many times spiritually flaky), and coaching is a subjective thing.]

Professionalism
- through certification (the purpose of this class)
- through standards
- through belonging to the IAMC (International Association of Marketplace Coaches), or a similar network

Accountability
- through relationships and regular reporting or checking in
  » with the intercessor manager
  » with you—via e-mail updates and/or sessions with you, your business team, and possibly your spouse
  » with others on your spiritual advisory team
- through the production of reports that come out of the intercession time with God
- through recorded, regular coaching sessions with you that are forwarded to your PLI

In addition, there is a feedback loop in which you can give the intercessor updates as to which things to stop praying for, along with new updates.

Say you are a pastor. Do you charge your congregation for each sermon that you preach? That would be absurd. Your congregation supports you for your time and the value of your ministry. So think of yourself as your SAT's supporter in the ministry to which God has called them and for which he has gifted them; you are paying for their time, the fruit of their relationship with God, and their giftedness.

We don't pay our pastors just to preach a sermon; their ministry is much more expansive than that, and so is the ministry of the PLI, the SC, and the CP. It's so much more than prayer; it's spiritual discernment, confirmation, encouragement, recording (via reports) what God is saying. It's warfare against the spiritual forces that are coming against you and your enterprise. It's devising strategies to defend against and prevent spiritual attacks. It's going ahead of the enemy in the Spirit.

Too long have we relegated spiritual ministry to being free and not dared charge for it.

My well thought-out and rehearsed answer to questions goes like this: "Well, you pay a professional pastor, you pay a professional missionary, so why not pay a spiritual advisory team? Are they not as important to God as a pastor?" Wait; come to think of it, don't ask that! *Keep in mind that you are not only paying for spiritual services, you are also covering our operational costs, management costs, hiring costs, etc.*

The truth is all these people *are* just as important, and so is the machinist, the janitor, and the CEO too! Our work is our ministry, period. We don't differ in importance to God, just in our function. The word "work" in Greek, the language of the New Testament, comes from the root word *avodah*, which is the same root word as for the Greek word for worship. We worship in church, and we worship in work and *through* our work.

Too long have we in the church thought of intercessors as consisting of only a group of ladies who have their mornings free, and who have met together for years on Thursday mornings. Our churches have not honored these ladies as intercessors, recognized or acknowledged which anointing(s) they had, trained them to further develop their gift of intercession, or had excitement about recruiting others—both men and women from all age groups and different segments of society— to join the prayer teams.

Intercession in the local church has appeared weak at best and a social club at worst. "Remembering you in prayer" may have meant only that your name is uttered on a list, one of hundreds on Thursday mornings, if the person reading names at that time didn't fall asleep! (Sorry, that wasn't nice.) So I am writing this to bring these intercessors, coaches, and prophets into the twenty-first century ministry and to combine their giftings (in business, art, education, or government) along with the spiritual gifts to complete the kingdom company model.

Your SAT is like the hidden treasure

"For Scripture says, 'Do not muzzle an ox while it is treading out the grain,' and 'The worker deserves his wages'" (I Tim. 5:18).

"We always thank God for all of you and continually mention you in our prayers"
(I Thess. 1:2).

"And the people came to Moses and said, 'We have sinned, for we have spoken against the Lord and against you. Pray to the Lord, that he take away the serpents from us.' So Moses prayed for the people" (Num. 21:7 ESV).

"The kingdom of heaven is like treasure hidden in a field. When a man found it, he hid it again, and then in his joy went and sold all he had and bought that field" (Matt. 13:44).

> "Give the first and the best to sanctify the whole and the rest."
>
> — Robert Henderson, *The Caused Blessing*

Holy Spirit spoke to me, saying that those who operate in spiritual services are like the treasure buried in the field or assigned to *your field*—that is in *your* field of ministry, whether it is business, art, education, etc. When you find your SAT, you will do anything for them because you know they are the *key* to your breakthrough. They have been hidden just for you, and they are *tied to your land*, that is, they have the authority! If they do not know about your land (field), they will learn, but God has already given them that land. Therefore, do not let their giftedness remain buried any longer.

Be sure to train them about your organization and be sure the CRO or SC can meet your senior leaders. If you only have an intercessor, then this applies to him or her as well. The minimum recommended WISE SAT configuration is an SC and at least one PLI. Many times there are also CPs, the CRO, and multiples PLIs. Get an onsite assessment completed. (If you are taking the certification class, you will be given a sample assessment.)

Your SAT members are a treasure hidden in darkness. "I will give you hidden treasures, riches stored in secret places, so that you may know that I am the Lord, the God of Israel, who summons you by name" (Isa. 45:3). Only when they are found can their light shine forth. "Arise, shine, for your light has come, and the glory of the Lord rises upon you" (Isa. 60:1).

Money Is spiritual

God loves a cheerful (hilarious) giver.

Whatever we do, we "work at it with all [our] heart, as working for the Lord, not for human masters" (Col. 3:23). We give to man in the frame of acting as a channel to God.

God's promise of prosperity

Prosperity is not just financial success. Prosperity has within it the meaning of success at all levels in life: physical, emotional, mental, spiritual, etc. I am prosperous if I am doing the will of God and if there is peace in my marriage and family. As leaders, our job is to seek prosperity the way God has defined it for ourselves, our fellow leaders, our clients, and our families.

Why Should You Compensate Your SAT for This Ministry?

The tithe belongs to the Levite (pastor), and that special offerings such as firstfruits belong to the priest (the apostle). Otherwise, how can the apostle function (without finances)? If apostles go unfunded, it will lead to a diminishing of the apostolic work in the earth. When the seven mountains are properly aligned with the apostles, the church and all spheres of society will see great breakthrough. This is why WISE has adopted this model. Support is needed for this new function in the seven mountains.

- This is part of the reward for the coaches and intercessors, and it is given into the apostolic ministry. The apostolic ministry has the ability to fully reproduce its DNA. Scripture says that there are different levels of rewards or multiplication—some thirty, sixty, and hundredfold (see Matthew 13:23). The soil is important, and it is what produces the increase. The apostolic soil is the most productive. Not all ministries produce the same fruit, and God is calling on us to examine those ministries and to listen to God's voice as to where to give. Your WISE SAT members are good ground.

  > *"Modern-day Levites are pastors and modern-day priests are apostles."*
  >
  > — Robert Henderson, *The Caused Blessing*

- Remember, apostles bring breakthrough. Apostolic ministry has the ability to remove mountains, because it is largely assisted by the angelic realm and carries with it the authority of heaven (to make decrees). The apostolic ministry is preceded by meekness—power under control. Moses was a type of apostle, and he was the meekest man on the face of the earth (see Numbers 12:3).
- This is an ongoing relationship; you are not paying for an answer

or a breakthrough, but are supporting a relationship. Again, relationships are paramount. God wants to support you, but you must have wisdom. Desire the best for your SAT and love them, protect them, and pastor them. Then they will want to provide for you because the two of you are in covenant—many times for life.

- PLIs and SCs are on a par with church-paid ministerial staff.

The purpose of this book is to update and inform CEOs and other seven mountain leaders that there is a professional, certified level of spiritual expertise and involvement available within all seven mountains of culture. These trained personnel can operate in the local church, Hollywood, government, education, etc. in order to bless it. The main point here is about honor and expertise in making things happen for you and your enterprise.

This is a level of proficiency that deserves financial compensation and recognition similar to that of other church staff and professional positions. For too long, the spiritual service experts have hidden out in the church. Now God is calling them into the light, and to—as the apostle Paul said to Timothy his son—"discharge all the duties of your ministry" (II Tim. 4:5).

Contract versus covenant

The world understands contracts. If one party fails to uphold the contract, just break the contract and pay a price. Covenant is God's way to do things. It is God who ultimately upholds his part of the covenant by providing results, but we must pray, war, prophesy, decree, and believe.

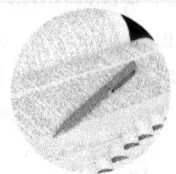

While there is a contract between you and your SAT, the basis of that covenant is that God is the third person involved.

God takes a contract very seriously. The seven mountains require and expect professionalism, so contracts are vital. They reflect the earthly reality of a spiritual committment.

Money is spiritual. "For where your treasure is, there your heart will be also." (Matt. 6:21)

God wants to intervene in your life, he wants to solve your problems, and WISE has the ability to serve you in every area of spiritual need. That's the essence of what we do with spiritual services—we come alongside and show our clients that they are not alone. We do life together as family. Even if you do something wrong, as long as your desire is to please the Lord, God loves you and does not judge you; he can get you back on the right path. You and your team will decree a thing and it will happen. "Surely then you will find delight in the Almighty and will lift up your face to God. You will pray to him, and he will hear you, and you will fulfill your vows. What you decide on will be done, and light will shine on your ways" (Job 22:26-28).

God allows the problems in people's lives for a reason. You may not have a business problem, but rather a marriage problem that God wants to work on. God can have a hook in us—his sons and daughters—and he may need to work on a specific issue; that is why he is allowing you to experience what you are going through. I promise he is being redemptive in allowing this, and your end result will be better than your beginning. In another sense, *he* is the fish with the coin in *his* mouth—the coin that solves *your* problem too.

SAT members are on the frontlines of the spiritual battle, and as such, need prayer cover. As intercessors and coaches, we see the need to have professional intercessors praying for us; however, we encourage our clients to also pray for us. When you pray for us, it is a blessing for you. We do not let you totally outsource prayer, because you will be robbed of a blessing if you do. We pray reciprocally for you, and vice versa, because we are family. As you will see, I do not shy away from being amply rewarded for my efforts, because many times what we do is the *key* to your breakthrough.

We establish a baseline and a benchmark that recognizes and rewards those trained.

The fact that this industry can be very prosperous comes with a price that must be paid in spiritual warfare, humility, travel requirements to our clients' sites, and the accompanying physical wear and tear on their bodies. For those of you who have been in spiritual warfare, you know it can be grueling at times. Their travel needs will be dictated by whether they are both coach and intercessor or fill one role, and by how large your enterprise is, what your immediate needs are, and how many leaders in your organization need ministry. As your SAT stands in the gap for you, your enterprises, families, and territories, you will see great breakthroughs. Any pain endured to see real change will be worth it.

God is waiting to bless you. What is needed is for your SAT to walk into your life. They are like a key to a door that has been locked. God just places the key (them) in the lock and turns it to open the door.

Why Do We Charge for Spiritual Services?

We have, in the past and also currently, given free services to many clients for many months . . . our reason being that we feel the Lord is telling us to do so, and/or we want potential clients to see the value of our services, and/or some cannot afford to pay for services at the time, yet they really need ministry, etc. Why not always give it away? That is the question many have in their minds. It originates with people being confused about the value of spiritual ministry and the separation of church and business. Which mountain supports spiritual ministry—the church or business?

Spiritual services add invaluable support to your enterprise.

We, as good church members, have focused on giving to God with our tithes and not on funding the pastoral staff or the church mortgage—this has been good for church leadership, but not so good for us. We don't associate that 5 percent of our tithe just went toward the preaching of a sermon or toward having the lights on for the Sunday morning service. There has been a lack of specificity regarding *where* our money goes. For example, when I was young I gave thousands of dollars to a well-publicized ministry. Did my money go for winning souls or for a fountain in the new building? *I don't know.* Our giving as Christians can sometimes seem to go into a black hole.

As a result, good church people are used to giving to God, but not to paying for specific, spiritually oriented services. Counseling is the exception, but counseling is not WISE's main ministry (even though counseling is a component of what we do). WISE is about relationship and honor.

How do you place a price tag on honor? This is the challenge.

There needs to be a *knowing* that you and your SAT have been placed together by God for mutual benefit, and that you need them in order to reach your destiny in God—not just in business, relationships, or finances, but in your *destiny*. Issachar speaks to this; tribe members honored and cared for their brothers and sisters in the other tribes. They lived to see the other tribes become successful and would fight anyone who stood in the way. You need your SAT to recognize and awaken your potential and calling in God.

This *cannot* be overstated. We have seen our clients grow and blossom into mighty men and women of God over the years. It's *your* time to do the same! It is a new day; welcome to marketplace ministry (and ministry in all spheres, not just in the church).

Honor

WISE exists to be an extension of the church for our businesspeople. Businesspeople are used to being the ones who write the checks and solve the problems in a church. Is the extent of their ministry ushering, or receiving the offering? Quite frankly, they are used to being prostituted; many pastors see their businesspeople as being provision for their own visions. Businesspeople are not generally honored in the church. Our number one goal as WISE intercessors and coaches is to honor and encourage our people.

Module 5: Endnotes

1. Pierce, Chuck D. and Robert Heidler. *A Time to Prosper, Finding and Entering God's Realm of Blessings.* Ventura: Regal, 2013.

Recommended Additional Resources

Books

C. Peter Wagner, *Prayer Shield: How to Intercede for Pastors, Christian Leaders and Others on the Spiritual Frontlines* (Prayer Warrior Series)

Robert Henderson, *The Caused Blessing: Connecting to Apostolic Power Through Strategic Giving*

Bill Hamon, *Prophetic Scriptures Yet to Be Fulfilled: During the 3rd and Final Reformation*

DVDs/CDs

Randy DeMain's sermons on the Sons of Issachar, www. kingdomrevelation.org

People

Robert Henderson, Robert Henderson Ministries
www.roberthenderson. org

Randy Demain, Kingdom Revelation Mnistries
www. kingdomrevelation.org

Bill Hamon, Christian International Ministries Network
www. christianinternational.com

Spiritual Coaching

"Pastor Charles prayed prophetically over my wife and me in February 2009. Among many personal words of the Lord that were received and clarified throughout the year, there was a word given about our investment business, Kingdom Legacy Fund. The Lord spoke through Charles and indicated the fund would have returns of over 100 percent, and even up to 800 percent coming. I must admit, my mind didn't really grasp those levels of returns as our best year was 18 percent, and the worst ever was just over 12 percent; we considered those to be good enough for anyone.

As I prepared for strategic planning for 2010 by just doing some number crunching, I calculated that we had increased capital to invest by 846 percent, and the annual return for 2009 was 100 percent better than our best year—18 percent in 2002 to 36 percent in 2009. The numbers didn't translate in my mind as earnings, but they did translate into impact for our company and for our clients. We are grateful to WISE for its continued prayer for our business, clients, and principals of Kingdom Legacy Fund."

— John M., Fort Lauderdale, FL

6

"Not by might nor by power, but by my Spirit, says the Lord Almighty" (Zechariah 4:6b).

Ministering to Leaders and Their Unique Needs[*]

You have unique responsibilities and pressures as a leader running an enterprise (such as a business). Things happen. You have to stay on top of every obstacle that comes your way—meet payroll during difficult times or shortfalls, deal with an IRS audit, cover the loss of two leaders who give their notices at the same time, attend to a lawsuit, all within the space —of a few days ... need I say more? WISE-certified spiritual, life, and executive coaches are aware of this, because many of our personnel have owned and operated organizations themselves.

We all need someone to give us permission to be whom God has called us to be.

We understand your pain in this highly competitive global marketplace, and we ask the Lord for a Romans 12:15 "rejoice with those who rejoice and weep with those who weep" baptism and identification with you. Until we identify with you and your leaders, the Lord may not give us glimpses into your heart and struggles. That type of insight is essential before we can weep between the porch and the altar, as a modern-day priest, for you.

"Let the priests, who minister before the Lord, weep between the portico and the altar. Let them say, 'Spare your people, Lord. Do not make your inheritance an object of scorn, a byword among the nations. Why should they say among the peoples, "Where is their God?"'" (Joel 2:17).

---

[*] For some of the specific areas we can pray for you, see the section called "Eight Powerful Prayer Shields" on page 29.

Frequency

We ask that our intercessors pray for the time recommended per week. You set your own schedule, but make sure it is not just all on one day. This keeps the coverage smoothed out.

> *"Surely the Sovereign Lord does nothing without revealing his plan to his servants the prophets"*
> (Amos 3:7).

Those of you seeking spirtitual services for your enterprise(s) may have many questions you want answered.

How can I know that my business or enterprise has the favor of God?

Can we receive the results that we would like?

Will doors be opened to new business without us having to do it via our own efforts?

Can families of leaders be at peace? Can employees be at peace with each other?

Will financial doors be opened?

Will God still prosper us in the midst of attacks—whether verbal, gossip, slander…?

Is the enemy resisting us, yet unable to stop us?

Is our faith being tested?

Does God care about my enterprise? Can God be involved with my enterprise above and beyond just blessing it in some general amorphous sense?

What hidden dangers exist if I am passive in my Christian walk toward my enterprise?

What if there are hindrances that I am unaware of? Can my enterprise be healed and set free from these hindrances?

I feel like I am walking the tightrope right now. What can I do?

What part do I play in the success or failure of the enterprise as its leader?

How can my enterprise be a powerful tool in the hands of the Lord in its own right?

I am not sure that I can continue if things do not change. Is there help?

The answer is YES! Let us help you in the way we have helped hundreds of others. There is hope!

The Importance of Revelation

> *"We are 'birthers' for God. The Holy Spirit wants to 'bring forth' through us. Jesus said in John 7 : 38, 'From his innermost being shall flow rivers of living water.' 'Innermost being' is the word koilia, which means 'womb'. We are the womb of God upon the earth. We are not the source of life, but we are carriers of the source of life. We do not generate life, but we release, through prayer, Him who does."*
> — Dutch Sheets, *Intercessory Prayer*

When the intercessor or coach does not have proper revelation, the tendency is to be overly flattering or overly judgmental or corrective in his prayers or comments. Watch out for this. "Surely the Lord God does *nothing* unless He reveals His secret counsel to His servants the prophets" (Amos 3:7 NASB, emphasis mine). I call this aspect of the prophetic for our clients "real time prophetic." We ask and God immediately answers, giving future direction, clarification, confirmation, etc. Many times it happens in our weekly or biweekly coaching or intercession calls or in spiritual staff meetings. God can surprise us, but know that when he speaks, it is irrefutable.

One time, one of our clients (early after the establishment of WISE) asked us what the next investment project was for him. He was a hard money lender for residential rehabs. God immediately spoke to me and told me that it would be a hotel, and he was astonished because this was not even remotely on his radar. However, two weeks later he got a call out of the blue about a hotel that was for up for sale. Had God not *intervened*, then he almost surely would have turned the deal down, but God wanted him to finance that deal.

God knows our future! God knows your future. Being able to hear God's voice is paramount in this new industry.

I cannot overly stress the importance of being able to hear God's voice *for yourself*; this is an ability that all of God's children need to have. (In John 10: 27 Jesus said, "My sheep listen to my voice; I know them, and they follow me.") I also cannot over stress how important it is for you to cultivate the ability to hear the voice of God, and WISE can help you with this.

There are gifts of Holy Spirit[†] outlined in I Cor. 12 and I Cor. 14 which mention the revelatory functions of Holy Spirit, such as the word of knowledge, word of wisdom, and discerning of spirits. These gifts, combined with the gift of prophecy (which we are actually told to covet in I Cor. 14:39 KJV, and to "desire earnestly the best gifts" (I Cor. 12:31 KJV) of which prophecy is at the forefront), creates a prophetic flow. This prophetic flow is divinely powerful in providing revelation and confirmation, and in answering questions.

> **Specifically, prophetic flow gives revelation about:**
> - what's-next type of questions [real time prophetic (RTP)]
>   » "What is God going to do?"
> - global, overall, general company direction
>   » "What should we do?" and
> - God's in-depth knowledge about our lives and situations.

Prophetic flow reminds us that God cares about our businesses and our livelihoods and wants to *invade* our enterprises (but he will invade our enterprises only with our permission, since Holy Spirit is a gentleman).

Interceding in this way is very closely related to the real time prophetic ministry (RTP) mentioned previously. Intercession and RTP work together. You cannot have one without the other, and when used together, the quick revelation as to what is wrong or what is needed, followed by the apostolic decrees and prayers to get the job done, are priceless to you.

Can you see how powerful this is? RTP enables us to be in direct communication with God and to enable quick answers, strategies, and solutions. Remember that when you are interceding, there is a difference between knowing what the problem is, knowing what to rebuke in certain situations, and then in commanding the breakthrough. This is a three-step process, not just a "God, answer my prayer" process.

A final thought for this section—notice we don't just ask God to bring the breakthrough. He says, "You do it."

[†] Before I continue on this subject, I'd like to clarify my terminology for Holy Spirit: I do not refer to him as *The* Holy Spirit. I don't call myself "*The* Charles"; I say simply my name, Charles. Holy Spirit is his name, he is not a thing, a "the" or an "it"; he is the most powerful spirit in the entire universe, a spirit whose name is Holy.

We command the breakthrough.

"Bind their kings with fetters, their nobles with shackles of iron, to carry out the sentence written against them—this is the glory of all his faithful people" (Ps. 149:8-9). God has given that authority to us—"the glory of all his faithful people." We are the enforcers of heaven's decrees, the ones who unlock the mysteries of unanswered prayer. Unanswered prayer and enigmas are solved, logjams are released by prophetic/apostolic intercession, and solutions are implemented by those in authority, all at our word. Sounds like an important job, wouldn't you say? Do you think there is more of a need for this ministry in our increasingly complex and interrelated world?

Spiritual Coaching

Spiritual coaching focuses on your inner life with God—your prayer life, worship times, and adoration times with God. The Bible is also emphasized, along with certain books of the Bible that highlight wisdom, salvation, and self-discipline. Spiritual coaching also helps "activate" you by idenitfying your unique makeup of personality, gifts, amountings, and dreams, and then emphasizing their use in everyday life.

Discover your ministry and weapons of warfare, the major gifts of Holy Spirit you operate in, the five-fold ministry gift(s) you have a natural bent for, and how it all relates to marketplace ministry in all seven mountains of cultural influence. Profile assessments are used throughout the process, such as the DISC and the spiritual gifts inventories.

Not only can an individual go through this process, but also the leaders and employees in the organization. It will better help them appreciate each other's gifts and talents and foster closer teamwork.

The WISE master offerings list has all of the services and trainings that WISE offers—coaching, intercession, inner healing, and counseling—as well as our spiritual gifts intensive trainings. Find out more about them from your WISE representative.

WISE coaching guidelines

WISE coaches are coaches first and a counselors second. I have coined the term "coachelor" for this. Traditional coaching models do not tie coaching in with counseling, it just tries to get to the end result or goal. but since you are a Christian, you know that there are spiritual roots to many issues in life.

Healing

Do you know that inner healing is the highest form of healing, even above physical healing? This is because it is eternal. It helps to be a healer—emotional or spiritual. God sends me many leaders with lifelong issues, and in every case he has set them free from their issues and distresses. It helps to have many different protocols and methods in one's toolbox.

I have been a student of healing strategies and techniques, and I am always excited to learn new tools to add to my arsenal. Your coach may be experienced in several healing modalities, to your benefit. Most of our WISE reps are inner healing and coaching veterans, and some are both licensed counselors and coaches, such as LPCs or LMFTs.

Coaching gets you through roadblocks to reach goals and healing gets you to the root problems of *why* your goals are not being met, which is critical. Why are you stuck? What is limiting you? How does your view of God, yourself, and others affect your day-to-day life? Self-limiting behavior needs to be addressed, so we always start out our serious clients with the "Restoring the Foundations"‡ method of inner healing and then move into "Healing the Brokenhearted"§ and prophetic deliverance (similar to Sozo).¶ Ask to see our Master Offerings List for descriptions and fees.

God's leaders have issues

Almost of all God's leaders have issues that they are dealing with, mostly behind the scenes. Why not get rid of those problems, such as childhood memories, intimacy and communication problems in your marriage, a wall between you and God, etc. We can help! Your

---

‡ See rtfi.org
§ See kathioates.com
¶ See bethelsozo.com

SC is trained to bring you freedom in these areas, thanks to our 7M Coaching Certification. The WISE model combines both intercession and coaching for this very purpose—to help speed along leaders all over the world in their spiritual development, both personally and professionally, with full confidentiality.

What Is a Destiny Link?

We are all born with innate spiritual strengths and weaknesses. We come into this world needing each other. We grow in life needing each other. At WISE, we call our need for others *destiny links*.[**]

Types of destiny links include:

someone sent by God to get you to your next assignment, or

a seasoned advisor who has already been where you are going, e.g., Jonathan and David, Elijah and Elisha, Paul and Barnabas

Each Enterprise Is a Spiritual Entity and Has a Destiny

An enterprise, whether profit or nonprofit, is a spiritual entity. It has a spiritual destiny to fulfill (from God). As God's sons and daughters, we are creators, like our Father. Organizations provide provision and sustenance for the owners and employees, but they also have a *social responsibility* to their regions and are to be giving centers. We believe that every organization needs to give a percentage off the top to worthy causes. This and other attributes are ascribed to *kingdom companies*.

When God places a creative spark inside a company's founder, it is because he has a *life* purpose for the company to fulfill—a spiritual blueprint[††] which encapsulates its destiny. This destiny may be unfolding; it may not be known in its entirety early on.

When God saved and called you, he put a destiny and a blueprint inside you with detailed instructions on what he has called you to do on the earth. One of these outworks is your enterprise(s). (I don't just call it a business, because we could be talking about a studio, political office, family, classroom, TV or radio station, church, etc. Each one of these examples is a part of God's—now man's—creation, and is a part of the kingdom of God if it has been properly dedicated and commissioned by God.)

[**] a term coined by Sandie Freed in *Destiny Thieves*
[††] Mentioned on page 77, under the section titled "Spiritual Blueprint."

God Is Not a Slacker

Is it not amazing that you and I arrived on this portion of the earth in this time to fulfill part of our particular spiritual and business destinies together? God is so much more grandiose, and his processes so much more complete and lengthy, than that which we have even imagined. God is not in a hurry; he takes his sweet time! I just turned fifty as I write this, and as I look back at half of a century, I realize that God works much more completely, yet much more slowly, than I was led to believe when I was first saved. I can see how his second coming may not happen quite as quickly as I and others have thought and taught. That is not to say we should be slack.

> *"The Lord is not slack concerning his promise, as some men count slackness; but is longsuffering to us-ward, not willing that any should perish, but that all should come to repentance"* (II Pet. 3:9 KJV).

The next level

With WISE, God instructs us to get you to the next level, where you can see new things and realize new freedom and authority. I use the example: if you are at the F in the alphabet, and have already passed through the A through E, do not try to to "hop over" the letters to get straight to the Z.

> *We Christians always seem to want God to do it right now.*

God says to look at what the F looks like (fantastic, by the way), and gets you there through coaching. You plateau, and after a little while, God opens up the G level. Coaching is about taking you through a process, many times structured and many times unstructured.

Your needs will dictate this. There may be a time to go through the homework assignments and pre and post coaching surveys methodically (samples available in Appendix 3 and 4), and there may be a time to lay that aside and just join in what Holy Spirit is doing through your life.

You may be in tears and your coach lovingly sits with you in your pain and lets you know that you are cared for and that she is there for you. There may be other times you just *have* to tell your coach something that happened this week, and your coach celebrates the victory and enters into your joy in the session. You may have a breakthrough in which God gave you a deep revelation about your childhood. Romans 12:15 says to "Rejoice with those who rejoice and weep with those who weep."

This is what we teach our coaches

WISE coaches want to help you hear the voice of the Lord better for yourself. We instruct our coaches to ask you what God is telling you, to let God be in control first, and then let you be in control of the session second.

> A prayer: *Lord, help us all to discern the signs of the times, but also to be diligent—with the gifts and connections you have given to each of us and in the fulfillment of our callings.*

Chapter 6: Endnotes

1. Intercessory Tools taught by Elizabeth Alves and team leaders. "Intercessory Training." Intercessors International, 2005.

Recommended Additional Resources for Readers and Students

Books

Cook, Dr. Bruce. *Aligning With The Apostolic: Apostles And The Apostolic Movement In The Seven Mountains Of Culture* (Vol. 1-5)

Hamon, Bill. *The Day of the Saints: Equipping Believers for Their Revolutionary Role in Ministry*

Freed, Sandie. *Destiny Thieves*

Sheets, Dutch. *History Makers: Your Prayers Have The Power To Heal The Past And Shape The Future*

Goll, Jim. *The Lost Art of Intercession: Restoring the Power and Passion of the Watch of the Lord*

DVDs/CDs

Pierce, Chuck, Robert Heidler, Linda Heidler, Paul Wilbur and Chris Hayward, "Positioned for Advancement: Understanding the Tribes and Months." www.gloryofzion.org/webstore

Os Hillman, "Reclaiming the 7 Mountains of Culture Introduction." www.tgifbookstore.com

People

Chuck Pierce, Glory of Zion International
www.gloryofzion.org

Anthony Hulsebus, Dominion Ministries
www.dominionministries.net

Bishop Bill Hamon, Christian International
www.ChristianInternational.com

Groups

Christian Business Network
www.christianbusinessnetwork.org

Elizabeth Alves, Intercessors International
www.increaseinternational.com

A 7M-Enabled Leader

"I've only been with WISE for three months, but already see benefits. Prayers that I'd been praying for quite some time have been answered on the fast track. God is doing the work, but I believe he is pleased when his children partner together to come before him. I also appreciate WISE's interest in my family, as family issues can affect business. WISE's weekly counsel has been inspiring and thought provoking. If you're unsure as to whether to partner with WISE for prayer and support ... go ahead and take the risk...God honors our faith."

— Anonymous

7

"You will also decree a thing, and it will be established for you; and light will shine on your ways" (Job 22:28 NASB).

What Is Strategic Intelligence?

Before I discuss strategic intelligence "in our tagline," I want to talk about spiritual intelligence. We have heard of other intelligences, such as emotional intelligence.

Spiritual intelligence is the ability to ask and to know which spiritual forces and/or dynamics are in operation.

Is the source good or evil?

Is this a demon spirit, an angel, Holy Spirit, or a human spirit?

Spiritual intelligence also helps one know how to react and respond in a variety of situations, especially in professional situations.

For example, say a member of your SAT team (the lead intercessor, spiritual coach, or chief revelatory officer) is invited to a company board meeting. Spiritual intelligence is knowing when to speak and what to speak, given the varied audience of C-level people—CEO, CFO, CIO, etc.—as well as board members, who may not be known as well. As a rule, she should always be ready to respond when asked a question, or when asked for her perception or discernment on an issue, and take good notes. You, the CEO or chairman, were willing to take a risk in inviting her to the meeting, so we instruct our SAT tainees to be discrete and say few words, especially initially, and know their audiences. Being consistently involved at the board level is one of the highest honors in the spiritual services industry.

Strategic intelligence, for our purposes, carries with it all the ideas above, but it additionally has a *strategy* or *stratagems* for both the enterprises and for each individual product, service, or project the enterprises are engaged with.

Signs of the need for spiritual intelligence

You may be considering intercession because you feel as if something is lacking, but you cannot quite identify what is missing. Some possible explanations are: You have tried everything else and still find yourself lacking.

You wonder why some of your prayers, or the prayers of others, haven't been answered.

You have achieved a level of success in your enterprise, but wonder why you haven't gone to the next level.

You wonder why it seems as if you are caught up in the world's way of doing things and can't break free.

You lack a detailed roadmap of where God wants to take you and your ventures.

No one has been running interference for you and deflecting the attacks of the enemy.

No one has given you the spiritual intelligence you need.

You don't have a team that can listen to the chatter through advanced spiritual intelligence, such as the sample story in II Kings 6:8:

> "Now the king of Aram was at war with Israel. After conferring with his officers, he said, 'I will set up my camp in such and such a place.' The man of God sent word to the king of Israel: 'Beware of passing that place, because the Arameans are going down there.' So the king of Israel checked on the place indicated by the man of God. Time and again Elisha warned the king, so that he was on his guard in such places. This enraged the king of Aram. He summoned his officers and demanded of them, 'Tell me! Which of us is on the side of the king of Israel?' 'None of us, my lord the king,' said one of his officers, 'but Elisha, the prophet who is in Israel, tells the king of Israel the very words you speak in your bedroom.'"

You don't have a ministry team which immerses itself into your DNA and your company, one that seeks the Lord to understand the times and the seasons of your enterprise's impact through its products and services.

No one has ever given you permission to succeed or believed in you.

How can the local enterprise/establishment be as important to the kingdom as the local church?

God is "into" networks, and as such, your business(es), ministry, studio, governmental office, school, etc. can become a part of the regional, national, and international network of heaven. The fact that your enterprise resides on land and in buildings is hugely important. It is all about the land. Land and buildings have occupants at many levels, and both have a spiritual memory. We must take this into account when dealing with issues related to cleansing, as well as to armaments and fortification that the Lord desires to bring into a region or territory. God wants to use your property as a beachhead to minister to your region! He wants to use it as a regional apostolic hub.

There is authority in financing, manufacturing, and ministering to people. What a powerful tool is your enterprise in the hand of God! If you and your leadership are teachable and pliable, there is nothing God cannot do through the physical aspects of your company—it becomes a natural extension of heaven's spiritual effects. Again, it's all about the land. Every establishment can be an armament for the kingdom and part of the heavenly network—a launching point, which is just as important as the local church (but which differs in function) for God's angels to the territory and the region. Does this not excite you? It excites me! Put another way, God wants to use your lands and buildings for his purposes.

Spiritual blueprint

Strategic intelligence enables you to create a plan for success in the competitive marketplace of your company in the areas of marketing, sales, new initiatives, etc. This level of involvement is usually made at the CRO or spiritual coach level, but you need to be comfortable with this level of participation.

Battle plan

A plan that the spiritual coach or intercessor will have some involvement with is a battle plan. This is a strategic plan that addresses the issues and resistance, both within and without (outside) the company, and will be deliverable from the beginning. [The initial assessment is an on-site visit that includes interviews with key leaders, a tour of the facilities, "listening" (for spiritual chatter) in the offices, and other aids. The assessment helps to *diagnose* where the company has been and where God wants to take it. The assessment report is one of the deliverables.]

The battle plan is a strategic intelligence plan that addresses all resistance, territorial spirits, competitors, and issues that have to be overcome. The battle plan is a forward-looking document that consists of strategies and tactics in advancing the kingdom of God through the outworking of the enterprise.

Strategic intelligence has to do with how to respond to the plethora of spiritual, management, tactical, personnel, financial, and operational issues which can arise. Remember, every issue that the company faces has a spiritual component to it. Strategic intelligence has to do with what is really going on, not just the superficial symptoms, and how to respond to it. Again, this means getting to the root of things. Consider a doctor in the act of diagnosis. As he methodically examines the patient and takes note of the symptoms, he is able to reach a conclusion that may not be initially obvious to the layperson. 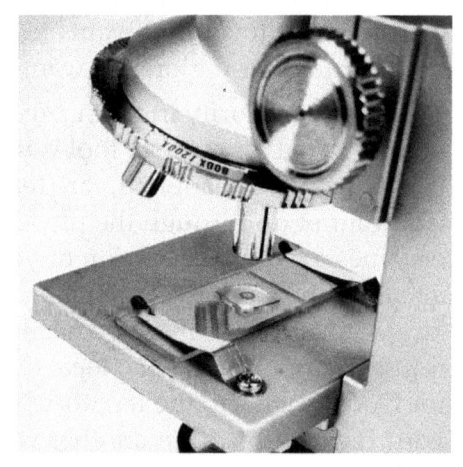 The doctor uses a number of diagnostic tools. Similarly, the spiritual advisor uses a number of spiritual diagnostic tools.*

Ten Things a Coach Can Do For You

The word coach has its origins in transportation—a conveyance to take you from where you are to where you want to go. That's exactly what we can do together. Einstein famously defined insanity as doing the same thing over and over again yet expecting a different result. If you're stuck, sliding backwards, or moving forward just too frustratingly slowly, it may be time to find a coach to mentor you, challenge you, and help launch you to the next level.

---

* We will address these tools in the certification class.

Here are ten ways that working with a coach can help you realize the best:

CHECK YOUR ALIGNMENT. One of the first things that a golf coach will do is make sure you are aimed at your target and that all of the fundamentals are sound. As your coach, I want to make sure that you have balance and that you are aligned with your purpose and connected with your calling.

CHECK YOUR BLINDSPOT. A coach can help you identify and remove some of the barriers that you may have in place that are keeping you from achieving your goals and realizing your dreams.

CHECK YOUR PROGRESS. By having someone to check in with weekly, you have a new level of accountability. Reporting your accomplishments and initiatives to your coach keeps you focused on the small steps that are required to reach big results.

LIFE ENRICHMENT. There's more to life than work. A good coach can help you understand a life plan, reduce the stress in your life, build a fulfilling balance in your life, and improve your relationships with others. He can help improve your self-awareness and consciousness, improve your self-discipline, point you towards God and motivation, and even improve your health, well-being, and happiness.

CREATE YOUR VISION. Your coach can assist you in understanding your strengths and how to play to them. You have someone who can help you get very clear about who you are and your core values, passions, and needs.

CELEBRATION AND ENCOURAGEMENT. Your coach will celebrate with you as you accomplish and step toward your personal definition of success. There will be times also when you'll need support, nurturing, and a source of energy to help you believe in yourself and achieve your dreams. A coach can help you turn setbacks into comebacks.

RAISING THE BAR. Constructive "challenge and stretch" goals can move you quickly to higher levels of achievement and prosperity. Your coach can identify new skills that you may need and provide you with resources and options for increasing your professional value.

COLLABORATOR AND CO-CONSPIRATOR. Imagine how much more confident you can be in your new ideas, creativity, and innovation when you've bounced them off a practiced, experienced professional who has worked through the challenges that you are now facing. A coach is a sounding board and veteran who can show you the shortcuts (that he learned the hard way).

NONJUDGMENTAL. You can tell your coach anything, things you wouldn't tell anyone else. Your coach is trained to be nonjudgmental and objective. She'll point out where your thoughts aren't congruent with your goals or values, and will share where she has seen those ideas work or not. You can try out any thought or idea, and together you can find what's brilliant about it and get rid of the rest (within a biblical framework).

PLAYING THE BOUNCE. We live in times of incredible change. Life brings surprises, setbacks, changing circumstances, and economic realities. Technology is a game changer at every turn. Your coach can help you see the big picture—the effects on your industry and your clients—and help you prepare for, adjust during, and bounce back from difficult times.

Many times both I and my client have agendas, but Holy Spirit always has his agenda for the meeting.

We want to be sensitive to your needs. You may have just been through a difficult situation and you need to talk about it with us.

Many times the Lord will allow you to be "triggered" so that the root cause of the issue can be healed cand dealt with.

Get Ready to Be a 7M-Enabled Leader

Alignment is critical and that is why God has brought WISE into your life. *How do you know when you are ready to step out and walk in this new authority?* Well, after you read this manual and go through the class, you will be informed and up-to-date on what God is doing to empower leaders to fulfil their callings and to employ spiritual technologies and strategies. Jesus's death paid the price for them and Holy Spirit has been sent to enact them on earth through you. Talk to your WISE representative and pray about the next steps.

So again, how do you know you are ready? You may have the finances, the training, and even the moxy, but how do you know that you won't be beaten up in the spirit? When the seven sons of Sceva (Acts 19:13-16) were casting out evil spirits, one spirit said something very interesting: "Jesus I know, and Paul I know about, but who are you?" This was directly before they beat up the sons and tore their clothes off. The enemy knew the authority of Paul and of Jesus, but these sons of Sceva were not proven in spiritual warfare, nor in having knowledge of the Lord. The Lord asked Moses "'What is that in your hand?' 'A staff,' he replied" (Ex. 4:2).

What do you have to work with?

You need to be able to assess your strengths and weaknesses as a spiritual and natural leader. The very fact that you have made it this far in this manual is evidence of a high level of spiritual hunger (or perhaps desperation), inquisitiveness, and developing maturity.

What gifts do you possess? What are your strengths?[†] WISE staff can advise and assist you by guiding you through some of our master offerings, like making a DISC personality profile and helping you identify your spiritual gifts. As mentioned previously, we can also help increase your ability to hear God.

Are you filled with the Spirit, with the evidence of speaking in tongues? Asked another way, do you have a prayer language? The baptism in Holy Spirit is the gateway into the supernatural.

Paul asked in Acts 19:1-2 "While Apollos was at Corinth, Paul took the road through the interior and arrived at Ephesus. There he found some disciples and asked them, 'Did you receive Holy Spirit when you believed?' They answered, 'No, we have not even heard that there is a Holy Spirit.'" (This is a subsequent and preferably coincident experience. Ideally, right after someone is saved he can be filled with Holy Spirit, but in my case, I received the baptism a number of months later.)

These and other questions need to be answered. Ask the Lord if you are ready. For many of you going through this course, the answer will be yes, and you will be delighted to have finally found a group like WISE to help release your kingdom company into its destiny.

[†] See Lifeway's "Discover Your Spiritual Gifts" survey at http://www.lifeway.com/lwc/files/lwcF_PDF_Discover_Your_Spiritual_Gifts.pdf.

> *If you do not feel ready, or if you do not have a peace,
> wait and continue to learn.*

Go over this material again, but do not be afraid of the enemy's retaliation if you proceed. The enemy can smell fear and is attracted by it. Fear will be the greatest obstacle for you and any other believer to overcome. It is the opposite of faith.

Fear will test your faith; conversely, you fight fear with your faith. Remember, "God has allotted to each a measure of faith" (Rom. 12:3 NASB). This is the measure that you will need in order to function and do what God has called you to do. You already have the faith, just learn to apply it and, like Peter, walk on the water to Jesus, who is calling you.

Personal testimony - not being ready

> A personal testimony of when I was not ready: When Liz was pregnant with Nathanael, I was heaven-bent on starting a church out of our home. We were not attending church and I had no covering. We had a handful of people to whom I was preaching and ministering, but we experienced oppression and spiritual warfare at a level I was not used to. I was dealing with the territorial spirits in the Tampa Bay area and was not ready for that warfare. My supervisor had just told me that we were going to rewrite the system that I had just spent eighteen months writing (as a computer programmer). Then Liz gave birth to Nathanael via a C-section and I had to take care of my new son. I was depressed; the church was not working. In addition, I was not sleeping. I felt alone. I remember complaining to the Lord, "No one believes in me." Right away the Lord said, "I believe in you!" Jesus came to me and said that he would never leave me. It was a great trial. It was during that time I experienced the benefit of one-on-one counseling. However, the little church folded. This experience helped me realize the importance of being properly aligned.

What Is Spiritual Alignment?

> Question: *Are you joined to and aligned with someone who has gone higher than you in God?*

Favor is transferable. Who walks in the favor of God and understands your calling, gifts, strengths, and weaknesses?

It is a *spiritual principle* that those who are aligned with or covered by an apostolic leader (very important) operate in the *same authority* of that leader. Put another way, those enemies who can be defeated by the apostolic leader can also be defeated by anyone aligned with that leader. Those enemies who come against anyone aligned with that leader also come against the leader himself. So there is the consideration of warfare from the leader's part as well, as far as who the leader is covering. The leader needs to know the people with whom he is aligning (who the leader is covering) fairly well, otherwise he may experience unnecessary spiritual warfare from people who are not properly aligned with *God*.

With whom are you aligned? Who is your apostle? Who can speak into your life, and who has gone further than you in the Spirit, not just in your specific calling as a seven mountains leader? Who can break things off of you when you need it? Who knows your calling and gifting; who can bless and commission you? WISE can be that for you, or you may have someone else you trust. Just be sure to have this person (or persons) in your life, someone whom you can bounce ideas off. It may be a coach—Paul had Barnabas.

Module 8: Endnotes

1. Transcribed from Elizabeth Alves and team leaders'. "Intercession Training." Intercessors International, 2005.

2. MacArthur, John. *Strange Fire: The Danger of Offending the Holy Spirit with Counterfeit Worship.* Nashville: Thomas Nelson, 2013.

Recommended Additional Resources for Readers and Students

Books

Vermaak, Natasha. *Repentance, Cleansing Your Generational Bloodline: Restoring the First Estate* (Vol. 1)

Hamon, Bill. *Apostles, Prophets, and the Coming Moves of God.*

Cook, Dr. Bruce. *Partnering with the Prophetic*

Website articles

Mike Parsons, "Gateways of the Spirit," www.freedomarc.wordpress.com/2013/11/26/gateways-of-the-spirit

DVDs/CDs/MP3s

Robert Henderson, "Operating in the Courts of Heaven" (Parts 1-4), www.roberthenderson.org.

Ian Clayton, "Supernatural Encounters 101" conference set. www.resources.sonofthunder.org

People

Dutch Sheets, Dutch Sheets Ministries | dutchsheets.org

Strategic Intelligence

The words were that God saw me as a knight in shining armor, and he was going to connect me with other significant people; I was going to have a turn of events and God was preparing a people for me to impart to and impact. That's the basis of the diagram, and I put it aside and went on with things, but at the same time Charles was saying to me multiple times to "hang in there until June; don't do anything drastic until June because something is going to happen in June."

What's happened is that your diagram was incredibly accurate! In retrospect it's amazing, and when I show it to people and give them the story behind it, the most common thing I hear is wow!

Here's what happened: We gathered all our forces and did a major effort to sell via our public seminars. To put this in perspective, three years ago we had approx. eight hundred people in these seminars, and this year the first six cities that we promoted in, which are cities where we have a good standing client base, we had a total of one registration. It was clear that God was saying that it was time for this to be over. We couldn't have tried to do that badly! There was supernatural involvement in this. I saw this as the turn of events which you had drawn in your picture.

I began searching for something else to do, and asking God what he wanted me to do. I was led providentially to a group called "Truth at Work," which organizes Christian CEO round tables. We're now going to be doing a video webinar round table with Christian CEOs meeting on a monthly basis, helping them grow their businesses and develop spiritually. I am absolutely convinced that this is the fulfillment of the words that you wrote down about God preparing a significant people group for me to impart to and impact. So...this all happened in June! We're talking about working with CEOs of Christian businesses around the country, and maybe even around the world, in these webinars.

I'm just here thinking Wow! This is incredible!"

— Dave K., Comstock Park, MI

8

"He said, 'LORD, you are the God of our people. You are the God who is in heaven. You rule over all of the kingdoms of the nations. Your hands are strong and powerful. No one can fight against you and win.'... All of the kingdoms of the surrounding countries began to have respect for God. They had heard how the LORD had fought against Israel's enemies" (II Chronicles 20:6, 29 NIRV).

Strategic Intelligence to Take and Integrate All Seven Mountains

LET HEAVEN INVADE
THE SEVEN MOUNTAINS OF CULTURE

WISE is developing strategic intelligence to take and integrate all seven mountains together. This will result in further enabling the kingdom of God in the earth.

Each mountain needs a specific strategy

The strategy to advance a campaign on the government mountain is totally different than the one needed to produce a Christian film on the arts & entertainment mountain. You may, likewise, see differences for each mountain in the type and severity of spiritual warfare to expect and in the strategy needed to win the battle for culture.

One size definitely does not fit all when it comes to the strategies for intercession, prayer, and breakthrough. There are some universal strategies for all mountains; notably the strategy of using Scripture, because God's Word always produces results. [We have included two appendices of Scripture for your use, divided into sections for the seven mountains. Appendix 1 contains Scriptures in a declaration format, and Appendix 2 contains Scriptures we have found useful for intercessory purposes.]¹

Okay. *I admit,* I just told you one size does not fit all mountains for intercession, prayer, and breakthrough strategies, but then *I immediately changed course* to say that Scripture can be a starting point strategy to reclaim any mountain. Don't get distracted!

> *In the 7M certification course presentation, I will list the specific strategies and thoughts for each of the seven mountains. In no way will the list be exhaustive; it is, in fact, constantly developing as I travel, meet new clients, and encounter new situations. I will tell you that we have been involved in all seven mountains, so our experience is ongoing.*

Some general principles* may make what I say here resemble the lighthearted three-part sermon outline—"I'm gonna tell you what I'll tell you, then I'll tell you, then I'll tell you what I told you." I've already stressed at least twice how important it is, as God's emerging general, to maintain an intimate walk with our Lord, and how he is the source to which you look for guidance for both you and your enterprise. In addition, you need to know how important these two spiritual disciplines are for you.

> *When believers obey the truths in God's word, and seek him for guidance and direction, even just one or a small group can make a major impact!*

In the strategies chart that follows, you'll notice that these two principles apply as valid strategies for multiple mountains, so they are listed at the bottom of the chart rather than for an individual mountain.†

Johnny Enlow says that the forces of darkness are at the summit of each of the seven mountains.‡

---

* in the *Change Agent* stories by Os Hillman

† A robust source of strategies to use for each mountain is found in Os Hillman's book, *Change Agent: Engaging Your Passion to Be the One Who Makes a Difference.*

‡ See my friend Johnny Enlow's excellent book *The Seven Mountain Prophecy* and, for specific strategies for the mountains, see *The Seven Mountain Mantle,* also by J. Enlow.

"Starting with Rosh Hashanah of 2015, a seismic shift will take place in the same way that the seven years of plenty ended in Egypt. If a great earthquake happens on that day, consider it the Lord's grace clearly signaling that earth-rattling changes are upon us. On this day, there will be a great unplugging of the systems of this world. The Lord will call for a famine on the foundations that are not sourced from His kingdom."

— Johnny Enlow, *The Seven Mountain Mantle*

Johnny says we will see the systematic crumbling of the systems of this world, and goes on to declare the need for the modern-day Josephs to arise with solutions to avert or lessen catastrophes. I see the times as being similar to those in Noah's day—God will depose the enemy's seven mountain leaders who are currently set up, and in their place set up his Josephs. It is a time for new beginnings.

Let us begin with how the seven mountains of culture are connected. The goal is to develop a strategy for each mountain or sphere that you may be operating in, and give you a strategy to connect those spheres or mountains when appropriate.

Defining 7M interconnections

Family is connected to all of the other mountains and is the foundation for everything because it is the most basic relational unit.

- Education and government are interconnected.
- Arts & entertainment and media are interconnected.
- Business and religion are interconnected—e.g., WISE.
- Business fuels all of the other mountains with finances.§

We can see the sevenfold Spirit of the Lord reflected in these connections and, interestingly, could view these connections in the design of a menorah, where the middle candlestick is foundational and the other six candles are connected into pairs by the curved lines of the menorah.

---

§ See Os Hillman's five-minute intro video about reclaiming the seven mountains, stressing the business mountain's strategic financial position, at www.7culturalmountains.org.

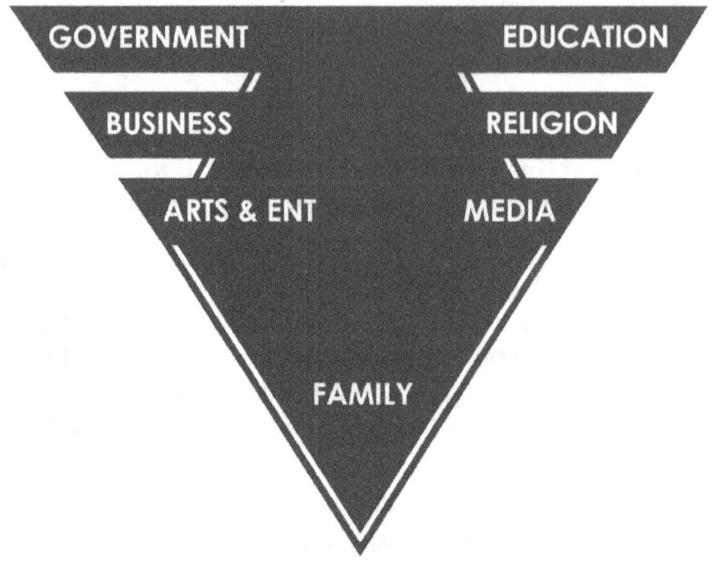

Isaiah 11:2 states: "The Spirit of the Lord (Adonai, in some translations) will rest on him—the Spirit of wisdom and of understanding, the Spirit of counsel and of might, the Spirit of the knowledge and fear of the Lord."

Family, connected to all the other mountains, is foundational, like the center of the candlestick, and it reflects the importance of love, as is the compassionate nature of the Lord reflected in the name *Adonai*. Wisdom and understanding could be seen as the connected mountains of business and religion; counsel and might could be seen as arts & entertainment and media (and could reflect the mighty power of media, with its control over "message.")[¶] The final pairing of knowledge and fear of the Lord could be seen as the connected mountains of education and government.

As you review the connections between the seven mountains, in light of the sevenfold spirit of the Lord in Isaiah 11:2, what does Holy Spirit say to you?

The Coming Seven Moves of God in the Mountains

The Lord has been speaking to me about the seven thunders

¶ We pointed this out in the text about going from intercession to intervention, starting on page 27 and revisited again as we speak about marketing in the next module.

in Revelation being connected to the seven mountains. The seven thunders are seven moves of God, one move related to each of the mountains. The scroll on which this was written was sealed up for the end times and then eaten by John; it was sweet to his mouth, but bitter to his stomach (see Rev. 10:9).

> Then I saw another mighty angel coming down from heaven. He was robed in a cloud, with a rainbow above his head; his face was like the sun, and his legs were like fiery pillars. He was holding a little scroll, which lay open in his hand. He planted his right foot on the sea and his left foot on the land, and he gave a loud shout like the roar of a lion. When he shouted, the voices of the seven thunders spoke. And when the seven thunders spoke, I was about to write; but I heard a voice from heaven say, "Seal up what the seven thunders have said and do not write it down." ... But in the days when the seventh angel is about to sound his trumpet, the mystery of God will be accomplished, just as he announced to his servants the prophets (Rev .10:1-4,7).

We are now in the days when the seventh angel is about to sound his trumpet! "Then the voice that I had heard from heaven spoke to me once more: 'Go, take the scroll that lies open in the hand of the angel who is standing on the sea and on the land'" (Rev. 10:8). The angel was standing on the sea (indicting humanity) and the land (indicating the marketplace). This is a move to *connect* the people to the marketplace and to *complete* the final work of God.

> So I went to the angel and asked him to give me the little scroll. He said to me, "Take it and eat it. It will turn your stomach sour, but 'in your mouth it will be as sweet as honey.'" I took the little scroll from the angel's hand and ate it. It tasted as sweet as honey in my mouth, but when I had eaten it, my stomach turned sour. Then I was told, "You must prophesy again about many peoples, nations, languages and kings" (Rev. 10:9-11).

Notice there is a *last days prophetic movement* coming which is related to the voice of the seven thunders, the content of which was *sealed up.*

The message of God in our day will be sweet (because we are speaking the exhilarating and fresh words of the Lord to each mountain) but in the outworking of it, the *digesting* of it, if you will, we—as God's Josephs—will have to endure the many shakings that are coming upon the world (but we will be victorious).

As the message continues in Revelation 10:11, "You must prophesy again about many peoples, nations, languages and kings." Notice many peoples (out of the sea), nations (sheep nations), languages and *kings* (indicating the marketplace). These seven end-time messages will be sent *to the entire earth* and to *all seven mountains of influence*.

Finally, John was given a reed and told to measure the temple (the religion mountain) (see Rev. 11:1). The implication is that this event was next in the sequence, *but it may not be*. My opinion is that it *is* next in the sequence of chronological events. The religion mountain is very important to God.

The book of Revelation next mentions the two witnesses. Their power is to defy death and to exact the wrath of God on the earth during the great tribulation, but there must be a move of God in each mountain beforehand! Maybe God will use *you* to prophesy and release one or more of these seven thundering voices, which are seven moves of God—one for each sphere or mountain of influence. Like John I say, "Even so, come quickly, Lord Jesus!"

The Tipping Point

Since 2000, Lance Wallnau** and Os Hillman†† have given many talks about the marketplace ministry strategy for taking the seven mountains (and have been talking about it more since 2009). Christians who desire to reform our culture have changed their strategy in order to honor the tipping point. Early on, the strategy focused on placing Christians at high points—points of leadership (affluence and/or influence)—in the seven mountains. A weakness

---

** You can find more info on Lance Wallnau at www.lancelearning.biz.
†† You can find more info on Os Hillman at www.marketplaceleaders.org.

of that strategy was that it could be a slow process (and often quite expensive) to place only a few leaders in high places. We noticed that the morality of a company (or segment of society, such as a city agency) could not be dictated downward to those working at lower positions.

Another aspect of societal change offers more promise for easier and, perhaps, faster results—the aspect of a tipping point. Missionaries have observed this phenomenon. Although it takes only a small percentage (4 percent) of leaders to create an appreciable influence on a segment of society, it doesn't take much more of the grassroots population (a little over 10 percent) to influence one. Currently, those Christians who desire to reform all seven segments (mountains) of society are shifting their foci to concentrate on creating tipping points. They are focused now on making more disciples at the grass roots level on each mountain rather than placing a few Christians in high areas of affluence and influence. The result can be to, essentially, tip the mountain over through the influence of that critical percentage of Christians exerting their grass roots influence (enhanced by the spiritual power of our Creator).

What does 7-UP have to do with a tipping point? Well, picture in your mind the seven mountains of culture (business, education, media, etc.) tipped over so that the playing field of each mountain (the base) is now at the top, and a base of Christians have access to the mountain peak, not just the top influencers. We are turning things upside-down (right-side up), hence the term "7-UP."

How can a 7M leader interact with that strategy? God can use any business or enterprise as a change agent to help reform society. For instance, as you are mentored on godly time management, you place your first priority on quality time spent with God (which helps bring the insight and blessings God has intended from the religion mountain for you and your business, and empowers your success). As you place your second priority on time spent with your spouse, and your third priority on time spent with your children, you honor God in a way that creates ripples of blessing in the family mountain. As you continue to align your priorities with God's priorities, you put your organization at the next (fourth) area of priority, which is in the proper position to receive the tangible and spiritual blessings God ordains for your business.

What is a tipping point?

A critical juncture, a defining moment in a series of events (think economic, cultural, social, etc.,) at which time a series of significant, often momentous and irreversible, reactions occur. We are at many tipping points in society: governmental, financial, economic, spiritual, etc.

> *You were created to be a world changer and history maker. You are needed.*

Spiritual life coaching - a new kind of tipping point?

All spiritual life coaching is not created equal! There are at least three broad approaches to coaching based upon one's worldview. The first is a purely secular approach that attempts to unlock the person's human potential. Techniques used may be such methods as NLP, etc. The second takes a non-Christian spiritual approach to "enlightenment," and may be combined with the first. It harnesses components of the New Age movement, such as the divine nature being present within the person who has not acknowledged Christ. The third is a Christian approach, which utilizes the God-given gifts within the person and acknowledges the need of Holy Spirit in achieving greater results.

All spiritual/life coaching is *not* the same; it can incorporate elements of humanistic and new age teaching. We believe that the human spirit can only achieve enlightenment and actualization through a Romans 12:2 transformation of the mind after a true born-again experience.

This coaching is combined with the knowledge of God's perfect will for you. We tap into your gifts, which will propel you into accomplishing your destiny. This is called being in the flow—that feeling of being 100 percent alive and operating on "all cylinders," if you will.

Life coaching *is the foundation of what we do as coaches, and deals with the basic issues of life—relationships, goals, personal issues, hang-ups, etc.*

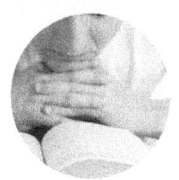
Spiritual coaching *deals with your inner life and relates to your walk with the triune God. In this discipline, we help you to better hear the voice of God, to relate more deeply to the godhead, etc.*

The WISE approach to coaching is as follows:

Many Christians are prone to live and experience their Christian walk through head knowledge. We help people relate to the Lord and to each other at the heart level. What are your relational skills? How can you improve them?

WISE asesses your greatest needs (as well as your spouse's). We do a temperament profile—to assess your personality and further understand who you are, how God made you, and how you relate to other people.

Our inner healing includes looking at four main areas of blockages, spirit/soul hurts, sins of the fathers, freedom from spiritual oppression, and identifying and reversing ungodly beliefs. Where are the gaps in your goals? We coach to them. Where are your blind spots? Over time we address them.

WISE spiritual coaches have a strong business foundation and spiritual background that help jumpstart your personal, spiritual, and professional goals. We help you, through the power of the Holy Spirit, to fulfill them. How would you like someone in your life that keeps you accountable to your goals, someone who personally cares for you and is not afraid to address issues that you may or may not be aware of?

God creates each of us with inherent strengths and weaknesses which he uses to develop us into mature Christians. God wants you to be a lover of truth. If you are determined to walk in truth and shun deception (through ungodly beliefs about yourself, God, or others), to get the victory over long-standing issues in your life, to be challenged to go to your next level, or to have a sounding board for you spiritually, then you need a coach. If you want someone who will train and challenge you to hear the voice of the Lord better, or who can provide prophetic input into business decisions, a WISE spiritual coach may be just what you need. On-site visits and regular meetings help to establish a growing working relationship.

Transformation

The Lord is raising up modern-day Josephs and Daniels and those like the sons of Issachar who "knew what the times demanded" (I Chron. 12:32). We believe that God's angels and anointing will be available to strengthen and empower you to finish the race that is before you.

God can show you the technology, healing, demographic, and spiritual waves that are coming and how to respond to them to get his people ready. He is going to show you the new economic super cycles that are coming, the new trends, and new inventions.

A major blessing an SAT can be to the business community is in its ability to help each owner transform his enterprise into a kingdom company. WISE can partner with you to create a kingdom company and bring it everything it needs to function in its destiny. You are one of the Josephs and Daniels of the twenty-first century and we are here to serve you.

> *Now your business has the opportunity to be realigned from its foundations up, and you may have an enterprise that can serve and change the nations.*

Module 8: Endnotes

1. Gladwell, Malcolm. *The Tipping Point: How Little Things Can Make a Big Difference.* New York: Back Bay Books, 2002.

Recommended Additional Resources for Readers/Students
Books

Hillman, Os. *Change Agent: Engaging Your Passion to Be the One Who Makes a Difference* [which contains a chapter for reclaiming each of the seven mountains, and relates stories of successful culture change, often by a single change agent or small group, and the strategies used to accomplish those successes].

Enlow, Johnny. *The Seven Mountain Mantle*

Ferguson, David. *Top 10 Intimacy Needs* (Intimacy Monograph Series)

Femrite, Tommi. *Invading the Seven Mountains With Intercession: How to Reclaim Society Through Prayer*

Wallnau, Lance, and Bill Johnson. *Invading Babylon: The 7 Mountain Mandate*

Cook, Dr. Bruce. *Partnering With The Prophetic: Portfolios, Protocols, Patterns & Processes*

DVDs/CDs/MP3s

Os Hillman. "Reclaiming the 7 Mountains of Culture Introduction." DVD. www.tgifbookstore.com.

Lance Wallnau. "The 7 Mountain Mandate: Impacting Culture Discipling Nations." DVD. www.morningstarministries.org.

Os Hillman, Lance Wallnau, Johnny Enlow, and others. "7 Mountain Strategies: Keys for Cultural Influence." Audio CD Series. www. tgifbookstore.com

Website articles

Os Hillman, TGIF Daily Marketplace Devotional, www.marketplaceleaders.org/tgif

Videos

www.TippingPoint.TV

People

Os Hillman, Marketplace Leaders
www.marketplaceleaders.org
and his TGIF bookstore www.tgifbookstore.com

YOUR CHOICES

"I have been blessed with WISE Marketplace Ministries. I have enjoyed our prayer times, meetings, and prophetic words. I also have been blessed by the intercessor who was assigned to us and the details of her prayer times, which she e-mailed to us. This has blessed me to see the type of prayer going on behind the scenes. May God richly bless WISE and open new doors to new businesses."

— Daniel G., Austin, TX

"Charles and Liz have played a major intercessory role in my personal journey. In this end-time season, it is absolutely critical that the arrows of intercession we shoot hit the mark all the time."

— Patrick Kuwana
Founder, Crossover Transformation Group
Johannesburg, South Africa

9

Coaching introduction

There are three main areas of coaching as discussed in the introduction to this course—life, spiritual, and executive-level coaching (which is further subdivided into executive business and executive leadership coaching).

Executive-Level and Executive Leadership Coaching

In this discipline we deal with helpful tools for the leader's life such as time management, leadership development (both for the executive and for his or her team), communication styles and methods, 360 evaluations, etc.

Executive coaching is becoming more of an integral necessity for executives in leadership roles.

Coaching often relieves the loneliness at the top, which CEOs and their counterparts experience when dealing with the complex issues resulting from their decisions and actions. Egos, ethics, and perceptions that ultimately influence the stakeholders of a company require the introspection executive coaching can bring.

Executive coaches can address needs in leadership development, speech delivery, business etiquette, people skills, management, and even appearance. It may be necessary to have coaches who specialize in these different elements.

Why senior executives hire coaches as consultants

To observe their performance and give feedback. Impartial feedback is less threatening from a consultant coach.

Time and attention of the coach is devoted solely to learning and gaining new knowledge about the leader and the impact of the behavior changes on others.

Coaches must have an appropriate business background, be experienced in coaching skills, and be able to administer appropriate assessment tools.

Coach certification guarantees a specific level of competence. This is the purpose of our 7MCPC certification.

What the Executive Coach Can Teach

We can teach all of the following:

- ✓ How to communicate more effectively
- ✓ How to deal with the stress of changing environments in the company
- ✓ How leaders can become helpers, not just critics
- ✓ How to avoid and/or deal with confrontation
- ✓ How to focus on teamwork and positive reinforcement
- ✓ How to overcome internal barriers and strife
- ✓ How to develop delegation skills
- ✓ Management of issues related to business relationships
- ✓ Effective time management
- ✓ How to develop an effective leadership style
- ✓ How to create guidelines for moving up the ladder in the company
- ✓ How to develop and maintain a professional image and personal style
- ✓ How to walk in authority
- ✓ How to walk in credibility with a professional image
- ✓ How to deal with a lack of self-confidence
- ✓ How to strengthen stress management and coping skills
- ✓ How to create credible presentations
- ✓ How to share the leader's vision for the organization with employees

Business Consulting

WISE certified coaches are experienced in running an organization and are assigned based upon your mountain of influence. He or she can help you with marketing, social media exploitation, accounts receivable, information technology, etc. WISE also offers our "Extreme Company Makeover," which guarantees to save you 20 percent on your operational budget. Please ask your SC for more information and for our master offerings document. For class members, we cover the range of WISE offerings.

Initial consult

To request an initial consult with WISE do the following:

1. Fill out our two surveys online:
   - » https://www.surveymonkey.com/s/KTZVT78
   - » http://www.coachmybusiness.com/contact.php
   - » *Be sure to stay on the page after clicking submit. Then fill out the important questions and click submit again.*
2. To pay the $150 initial consult fee, use the donate button at the end of our home page.

WISE Ministries International

Workplace. Intercession. Support. Empowerment.™
Focused and Targeted Strategic Intelligence

WISE Ministries International is helping birth the spiritual services industry. it is a pioneer in the new "strategic intelligence" space, otherwise called "coaching and intercession for enterprises." Dr. Charles and Liz Robinson founded WISE Ministries International in 2005 to be a training, equipping, and service ministry to businesses, ministries, and enterprises in all seven mountains of culture. WISE provides intercession, kingdom consulting, and timely prophetic words in all seven of the spheres of culture, sometimes referred to as the seven mountains of culture: business, government, arts & entertainment, media, education, family, and religion. WISE services provide a vibrant training, consulting, and healing ministry for developing and equipping the body of Christ to live in victory through experiencing the delivering power of Jesus Christ, our Lord and Savior. WISE teaches people how to incorporate prayer into their enterprises, and trains and imparts into the next generation.

WISE is active in:

Government - by supporting local and national candidates, by impacting the governmental mountain through DC-based intercessory teams, and through its Gates2DC.com ministry;

Arts & Entertainment - through the Gates2Hollywood.com ministry and association with several major Christian film studios and releases;

Family - through its marriage counseling ministry;

Education - through its ministry at foundational universities, such as Harvard University;

Business - through entrance, via intercession and/or coaching, into over one hundred companies in numerous industries;

Religion - through support of church and parachurch ministries; and

Media - via Internet; via satellite—the On The Way Network and Cross Network, which covers the globe, with access to over 120 million people.

WISE employs intercessors and coaches all over the world in a decentralized model, utilizing the latest in Internet technologies, to teach people how to incorporate prayer into their enterprises.

WISE maintains offices in Hollywood, California; Austin, Texas; and Washington, D.C.; and we can also travel to enterprises for on-site initial consultations, assessments, and evaluations.

Licensing and Commissioning Leaders in the Marketplace

As a part of *our* commissioning, we (WISE) license and commission (we formerly used the word ordain) leaders in the marketplace.

> *WISE recognizes that God has called leaders in all the seven mountains, not just in the religious mountain.*

Accordingly, WISE recognizes that these ministers do not differ to God in importance as compared to those who hold traditional ministry positions in church, or who are supported by the church, such as missionaries. WISE further recognizes that those who have the ministry gift of apostle, prophet, pastor, etc. can function in their spheres of influence, i.e., in one or more of the seven mountains. WISE recognizes how vital it is, as a person progresses in his spiritual calling, to have a person or a group honor him and acknowledge his authority and sphere of influence by setting him in or consecrating him and being there as a guiding hand. If you or a leader you know could benefit from licensing (which is akin to a dating period for one year) or from commissioning, please contact our office to receive a list of requirements and benefits.

Confidentiality and Intellectual Property (IP)

We have been developing these offerings since 2005, and have touched thousands of people with this ministry. We know what we are doing. You can make a part-time or full-time income if you work with us, but please keep our processes, procedures, and intellectual property confidential. We require the two-year non-compete agreement so that if/when you separate from us you do not directly compete with us. It is better to work with us, as we can funnel work opportunities your way and handle the details so that you can grow your business, based on your preference of coaching and/or intercession. We provide a strong reputation in the industry, and are a spokesperson for it. In fact, we are one of its pioneers, continually shaping the industries of professional level intercession and spiritual, life, and executive coaching.

Overview of WISE Master Offerings

WISE provides a wide range of courses in personal development to WISE clients—in person, by telephone, SKYPE, and/or e-mail correspondence—through life, spiritual, and executive coaching in various areas and levels. We also offer courses for business transformation, and on how to assist leaders through transitions. WISE also offers personal ministry using spiritual and relational tools.

Certification Courses

WISE currently offers four certification courses in a series called "Let Heaven Invade the Seven Mountains of Culture."

Existing and planned volumes

Volume 1: WISE 7M Intercessor Certification Guide trains those with a calling to intercessory prayer to become seven mountains professional level intercessors.

Volume 2: WISE 7M Leadership Certification Guide informs leaders how to identify, engage, manage, and release intercessors, corporate pastors, spiritual coaches, and chief revelatory officers into their organizations for their corporate and personal well-being.*

Volume 3: WISE 7M Coaches Certification Guide (spiritual coach, life coach, executive coach, and executive leadership coach options).†

Volume 4: WISE 7M Chaplain Certification Guide is for corporate pastors or chaplains called to minister to an organization's employees.‡

Volume 5: WISE 7M Generals Certification Guide is for the top 7M marketplace leaders who need to deal with (take authority over and get to the root of) many situations which can arise in their global enterprises.§

Course schedule and format options

Certification courses happen monthly. All four of the courses listed above are available in two formats:

Group and Fast Track: Two-and-a-half days of live on-site training

Independent Study: All modules are divided over twelve weeks.

Both formats offer wisdom, and experience from WISE instructors.

Why certify as a WISE leader?

Reading this guide without participating in a live class or recorded sessions will prove to be valuable; however, if you wish to receive certification and full impartation (including proprietary material, sample forms and processes, etc.), you will need to attend the classes, or at least view the recorded version of the classes and complete the exercises.

You will be able to fully utilize and understand WISE's master offerings for you, your family, and your organization(s). Most importantly, certification will educate you on getting the most out of the spiritual services industry that WISE is helping to birth.

We hope you will align with us to see your destiny come forth.

---

* See marketplaceCEOS.com.
† See marketplacecoaches.com.
‡ See corporatepastors.com.
§ See marketplacecoaches.com.

About the Author

Dr. Charles and Liz Robinson have pioneered a global breakthrough in marketplace ministry through WISE Ministries International—a ministry that empowers leaders by providing a combination of business, spiritual, and prophetic support—using their impressive history of degrees and experience as a foundational guide. Both ordained ministers with the CIAN, and as current directors of the IAMIN, Charles and Liz maintain offices in Austin, Hollywood, and Washington, D.C. in order to personally minister on the mountains of business, entertainment, and government.

Charles is also the convener of the bi-annual Tipping Point Gathering 7-UP Unconference—an interactive three-day meeting of key leaders from the seven mountains of influence.

More From WISE Ministries

WISE Prayer Request Website and Theme song

WISE Prayer request site and theme song:
www.coachmybusiness.com/prayer-request.php

WISE Online Store Links for DVDs

DVDs from WISE (provided to Certification Course Students):

Intercession **2.0** http://fur.ly/ao8i

Taking **Company to Next Level Spiritually**
http://fur.ly/ao8if

Opening **Global Gates of Access and Provision**
http://fur.ly/ao8ig

Tipping **Point Media from WISE online store**
Tipping Point 2013 Gathering Conference DVD (also available on CD and MP3) http://fur.ly/ao8h

Our iPhone/Android Mobile App

As you move forward with your relationship with WISE, use our WISE app to submit your prayer requests, read our blog, find out where our next gatherings are going to be, or receive a prophetic word.

WISE Ministries International websites

Our main prayer websites:
sites:
    prayformybusiness.com
    prayformyministry.com

Our intercessor certification

    IAMCERT.com
    marketplaceintercessors.com

Our 7M sites:
    tippingpointgathering.com
    7mcouncil.com
    charlesrobinson.com
    7minstitute.com
    josephregistry.com

Our coaching sites:
    coach4mylife.com
    marketplacecoaches.com
    coachmybusiness.com^2

WISE provides monthly newsletters in "The Joseph Blog," available at:

coachmybusiness.com/marketplaceministry

The 7M book series is available at the site:
www.letheaveninvade7m.com

For information and to register for monthly gatherings, visit:
www.tippingpointnw.com

Site to purchase *Let Heaven Invade the Seven Mountains of Culture*:
www.letheaveninvade7m.com

www.ingramcontent.com/pod-product-compliance
Lightning Source LLC
Chambersburg PA
CBHW070922160426
43193CB00011B/1556